PRISONERS OF WAR
AND LOCALS

*Focussing on Wembury, Brixton and other locations,
including the Scottish link.*

Written by Maria Bojanitz
Published by Harebell

Printed in the UK. **ISBN 978-0-9553053-06**

Printed by Nick Walker Printing, Kingsbridge, Devon TQ7 1EQ. Telephone 01548 852812

Foreword

Several factors prompted me to compile Prisoners of War and Locals. My friendship with my parents was a strong influence and the link with their friends and acquaintances was an additional inspiration.

Having an interest in people and their part in local history I began collating recollections and other material in 1991. In addition to Wembury and Brixton, other places such as Dumfries and other locations came into the picture. Undoubtedly the collective story of the ordinary people adds a realistic dimension to history.

Maria Bojanitz
Mothering Sunday, 2nd April, 2000.

Dedicated to the memory of my parents Edna and Alfred.

My sincere thanks to the following people and establishments:

My mother Edna Bojanitz (nee Sly).

My father Alfred Bojanitz.

Johannes Löscher of Schwarzenberg, East Germany.

Heinrich Dennhoven of Inden Pier, Germany.

Salome Bünger (nee Dennhoven) of Inden Pier, Germany.

Alfred Neugebauer (my father's Godson) of Rentweinsdorf, Saxony, Germany.

Mr. Richard Folley of Brixton.

Mrs. Elizabeth O'Neil (nee Gosling) of Plymstock (formerly of Brixton).

Mr. Godfrey Smallridge of West Wembury Farm, Wembury.

Mrs. Mary Dyer (nee Towill) of Wembury.

Mr. John Casley of Cornwall, formerly of Hollacombe, Wembury.

Miss Barbara Snell of Hollacombe, Wembury.

Mr. Kenneth O'Connor and Mrs. Gwenda O'Connor of Wembury.

Mrs. Doris Russell (nee Congdon) of Plymstock.

Mr. Roy Roberts and Mrs. Ada Roberts (nee Steer) of Plympton.

Mr. Maurice Hammett and Mrs. Eileen Hammett (nee McCrum) of Plympton.

Mr. Hermann Beeck of Plymstock (formerly of Brixton).

Mrs Evelyn Osborne (nee Manley) of Plymstock.

Mr. John Truscott of Plympton for his information on trains.

Mr. Kimmo Kosunen of Wembury for his translation of some material.

Dr. Pam Soppet (Mrs. Bowring) of Rayleigh, Essex (formerly of Wembury) for her visits to Kew Records Office.

The Derwent Library, Dumfries.

The Barony Agricultural College, Dumfries.

The Public Records Office Kew for permission to reprint material.

The Commonwealth War Graves Commission.

The Evening Herald for permission to reprint archive news and photographs.

TocH

Nick Walker Printing for printing.

During the Second World War five Prisoners of War came from Kitley Prisoner of War Camp, Brixton, to work on Old Barton Farm at Wembury.

Alfred Bojanitz outside the camp nissen huts where the prisoners lived.

Cofflete Lodge
(Formerly Kitley P.O.W. camp)

Air raid shelter nearby

The child in this photograph is Mary Towill aged two. In the background we see Old Barton Farm as it was in the early 1940's.

Kitley Camp work party at Old Barton Farm, Wembury.
Left to right: Heinrich Dennhoven, Alfred Bojanitz, Johannes Löscher, Kurt Hollman(?), Karl ?

The wedding day of Lily Sly (Jnr) and George Harris (AC1 RAF) on June 20th 1942.

Lily and George were married in St. Werburgh's Church. This happy scene is at Hollacombe House. Recognized people in the photograph are as follows: In the back row: Eileen Drake (2nd left), church organist Mrs. Eliott (3rd left), Mrs. Spencer (5th left), wearing the flower is Bertha Avent (nee Steer ... cousin of the bride and her brother and sister, Bernard and Edna) (7th left), George Hammett (husband of Emma) (1st right), Harry Sly ... brother of George Henry Sly (2nd right), Irene Geach ... daughter of George Henry's sister Elizabeth Ellen Sly (3rd right).

On the steps: George Henry Sly (Snr) and his sister Emma Hammett. The lady in front of them is likely to be the groom's mother. Behind the bride ... her Aunty, Daisy Hornsby (nee Steer), and the groom's brother, and bridesmaid Edna (the bride's sister).

Above: circa 1928. The family Sly at Hollacombe House.

Left to right: Lily (Jnr), Lily (Snr) with Edna in front of her, Bernard with George (Jnr) in front of him.

Left: circa 1936.

Left to right: Edna, George (Jnr), Lily (Jnr).

George Sly (Jnr), June 1934.

George Sly (Jnr), June 1938.

Now, back to the German Prisoners of War who had been transported from Waterloo Station to Euston Station by army truck. The Euston line took them to Dumfries in Scotland (a long and tedious journey) from where they were taken to The Barony Camp.

In 1945 there were five or six nissen huts at Barony Camp. Today Barony Camp is an agricultural college.

The Barony Camp as it is today

Trains of the late 1940's and early 1950's.

Both these trains were to be seen on the Southampton line during the Second World War. The Prisoners of War are likely to have travelled on a train similar to the one in the first picture. This being The Lord Nelson 4-6-0 Sir Francis Drake Waterloo to Bournemouth, pictured here at Southampton Station in 1951.

A typical English army truck.

Of local interest, the young man in this 1939 photograph is my mother's brother, George Sly, who, along with his company, was lost in action when their munitions ship was bombed near Crete. George's name is recorded on the St Werburgh's Church War Memorial Plaque commemorating local men lost in action. My mother's face always lit up when she talked of George. She recalled him as a kind, warm hearted brother with a marvellous sense of humour.

My mother kept George's last letter home and all but two pages have survived.................

<u>2</u>

up here, everyone has them.
We are up the line a bit
and I expect you can guess
where abouts as its been in
the news a bit lately,
Although we are having a
quiet spell at present, but
I expect one of these bright
nights we shall have a
few visitors to drop us
a "present" or two, it seems
as if the Italians are a
bit windy after the duffing
up they got in their last
raid, the air force certainly
had a day out that day.
The raids we get here seem
so half hearted after what
we have seen in France

and Belgium, Jerry certainly
had guts, or was it dope.?
but we dont seem to be
able to make these chaps out.
I hope you have recieved
my letters posted on the boat,
my first letter arrived two
days ago it was from Maudie
so you can tell how welcome
it was after waiting so long
it was posted on the 24th
of August and I recieved it
Nov 11th, poor kid it knocked
her up a bit leaving without
even seeing her, but I must
say she took it well
considering.
She is keeping well up to
the time of her writing and

was expecting to start work
in a new ammunition factory at
her place so by now I
expect she is quite busy.
I dont know if she has
written to you or not, but
I know she is not fond
of writing, so Dad, will you
do me a favour and drop her
a few lines to cheer her up.
Edna will know the adress.
Well Dad & Edna I expect
by the time you receive
this letter it will be Xmas
so I will wish you all
the best even though it
wont be much of a time for
rejoicing but I suppose we
shall all make the best

The marriage certificate of George and Maude Clewes provides the following information:

They both were twenty years of age and were married in the district of Stoke on Trent on 23rd March 1940. Maude worked as a bar maid. George is listed as Private no. 835235, 16th Anti Aircraft Battery, Royal Artillery. On the certificate George's home address is Hollacombe House, Wembury, and Maude's home address is 39, Brookhouse Road, Meir Longton.

The Commonwealth War Commission further informs us that George died on Saturday, 26th April, 1941, aged 25. The son of George Henry Sly and Lily Sly. Husband of Maude Ethel Sly, of Hopton, Shropshire.

Included in the commemorative information of the Athens memorial in Greece, Face 3, we read the following:

Athens Memorial commemorates nearly 3,000 members of the land forces of the British Commonwealth and Empire who lost their lives during the campaigns in Greece and Crete in 1941 and 1944-1945, in the Dodecanese Islands in 1943-1945 and Yugoslavia in 1943-1945, and those who have no known grave.

Georgie in Alexandria.

The Prisoners of War produced a quarterly religious magazine at Barony Camp. Below is a copy of the front cover showing the artist's impression of Barony. This is followed by prints depicting the spiritual thoughts of prisoners.

14

The following reports of visits to the Barony Camp are reproduced by courtesy of
The Public Records Office at Kew

REPORT OF ENGLISH EDUCATIONAL VISIT OF MR. JAMES GRANT TO BARONY CAMP, DUMFRIES. NO.298
(formerly182)

DATE:November 8/9, 1945.

COMMANDANT: Lt. Col. G. Murray

STRENGTH: 1695.   Compound A 1205
                  Compound D 449

TEACHERS: 5.   ENGLISH PUPILS: 144   NO. OF GOS.: 144

TEACHERS:
    Compound A

    ARNO EIDNER (38) 1.5.07, B 129587, on previous report "B"
            Class: Beg. 30, Beg. 30.

    ALFRED LEONHARDT (43) 26.3.02, A 828238, on previous report "B"
            Class: Inter. 10

    HERMANN SCHÖNEFELD (40) 1.2.05, B 129800, on previous report "B/C"
            Class: Inter. 14, Inter. 10.

POW left in Compound B are now included in A; with them 1 teacher

    HANS ZAPP (38) 28.11.07, A 836131, on previous report "B".
            Class: Beg. 30.

Teachers previously listed in A and B and not now teaching:

    EMIL FAESEN - "B", EMIL STOEWER - "B", KLAUS LARSSEN- "B".

    Compound D

    JOSEPH KLEE (40) 1.3.05, B 32042, "B"
            School: Oberrealschule, München
            Univ. : München   100
            Pre-war occupation: chemist, München
            Class: Beg. 20
            Grading as teacher 2.

    KARL HABRICH (51) 13.3.95, B 31979, "C" - a fair speaker,would teach
if more pupils were enrolled.

    DR. KAPP, the Unterrichtsleiter,would like to have 10 copies of any advanced
text book for French and for English of the Velhagen and Klassing series.
He states that classics in English lie on the library shelves as the men have neither
the necessary taste nor vocabulary. He declared that modern novels of a light
type if sent to the library would hold their interest better such as
Warwick Deeping. He himself is too intellectual for this camp. His political grading
is"A".

    The atmosphere is friendly and peaceful. The buff cards having brought good
news on the whole, the Lagerführer says they have had a very calming effect.

    Music, at a very high level, is possibly the main interest in this
camp.

16

COMPOUND D:

With almost as many men as in the other compound there was only one teacher who taught 33 men. He is:

LARSSEN, Klaus (30): who learned English in the Realgymnasium, Köln, and was in the traffic section as a railway employee. Accent and pronunciation fair.
Tested: B.

I also met the man who is taking over the post of general Unterrichtsleiter to replace a man of great drive and with an enthusiastic following called FAHR, who had to be removed on moral grounds recently. His successor is
KAPP, Alfred (41), a doctor of philosophy of Heidelberg, a Mittelschullehrer in Heidelberg, who had some connection with the language side of the University. Of great self-assurance, he appears somewhat poisonous. The Lagerführer said he realised that he aroused great antagonism everywhere he went, but that there was no one wlse to conduct the studies. Kapp announced that he had classes of varying numbers of pupils, average about 10, in maths, chemistry, Greek, Latin, Chinese, Sanskrit and Russian, all apparently without textbooks.

CONCLUSIONS: The Lagerführer told me there were between 450 and 500 boys between 17 and 21 in the camp, and he was certain they were ready for some form of instruction. He said they had had no boyhood and were beginning to appreciate the lack of schooling , but he did not know where to begin, for lack of material and teachers.

There is a lack of energy in this camp on the re-education side. It could be stimulated by a series of lectures, I feel certain. The I.O. was to leave permanently on the Tuesday after my visit, and I have the impression that things will sink further still when he is gone. He is Capt. Gersin, who suffers from asthma and the usual lethargy it brings, but he has been interested in the men and helped them generally, and especially in forming an orchestra and obtaining musical facilities..

If ever there is a question of broadcasting to Germany from POW Camps, which I once heard mentioned, the choir of this camp is especially fine.

MR. JAMES GRANT'S VISIT TO BARONY CAMP, DUMFRIES.

CAMP 1021 298.

th 1945.

camp is immediately impressive on account of its size and the nature of its grounds. I was told that it takes a good hours' walk to go round the boundaries of the camp, which enclose two small lakes, beautifully wooded, on one of which are four swans and seven cygnets. The Officers' Mess is housed in a red sandstone mansion. The huts are scattered over the camp site as it was originally dispersed for camouflage purposes when it was an army training camp. All these facts make the camp most unusual.

The POW are divided into three compounds with open access to each other. There are three compound-Führers, but one of these is "primus inter pares", and arranged for the teachers and students to be brought together as I wanted to see them.

COMPOUND A:

Here there are five teachers and 93 pupils out of a total of 800 men. This is well below the average I have hitherto found in camps (15% to 25%). The teachers are:

(1) EIDNER, Arno (38): Learned English in the Realgymnasium, Borna Bei Leipzig. He was an official of a miners' Insurance Institute in Borna. He teaches
1 group of Beginners with 15 pupils,
1 " " Advanced " 10 "
Tested: A.

(2) FESER, Emil (43): learned English in the Oberrealschule, Wuppertal Barmen, was a bank clerk in the same town. Teaches 20 Beginners, and also History and Theory of Music. Accent fair.
Tested: B+.

(3) BRENNER, Paul (27): learned English in the Realschule, Herrenberg, Kreisböblingen, Wurtemberg. A savings bank clerk in Schwarzwald. Intended to train after military service in 1939 as a Protestant missionary.
Teaches 10 Beginners.
Tested A-.
Accent and pronunciation fairly good.

(4) LEONHARDT, Alfred (43): learned English in the Realgymnasium, Weimar. Was a commerceal school teacher in Rudolstadt, Thuringia. Teaches 10 Beginners, also Book-keeping, Commercial Arithmetic and Shorthand. Accent and pronunciation good.
Tested: A-.

(5) SCHONFELD, Hermann (40): learned English in the Realgymnasium, Berlin-Lichterfelde. Was a cashier and book-keeper in the Berlin University. Teaches 2 groups of Beginners with a total of 28 pupils; also Algebra and Geometry. Accent and pronunciation fair.
Tested: B+.

As can be seen from the foregoing, this compound is well served by fairly adequate teachers with small classes. Those I was able to see were teaching normal English with fair success. They were on the whole somewhat critical of GOS, which they used mainly to supplement lessons from Propellor and Linke, having one copy of each. They had a total of 40 GOS available. They appreciated the Directives, but asked for some reading material.

COMPOUND B:

Here I found only two teachers and thirty pupils out of some 700 men.. The teachers were:

(1) ZAPP, Hans (28): learned English in the Realgymnasium, Hamburg and obtained a diploma in 1929, after attending a six weeks course at Exeter. He was a textile business man in Hamburg, who had studied law for five terms at Hamburg and Munich. Teaches 15 Beginners. Accent and pronunciation good.
Tested: A-.

(2) STOEWER, Emil (19): learned English in the Oberschule, Lipstadt, Westfalen. Was a schoolboy till called up. His father is with him in this camp. Teaches 15 Beginners. Accent and pronunciation poor. A timid fellow.
Tested: B.

COMPOUND C: is not in use.

18

My father's Godson, Alfred Neugebauer, kindly wrote to Fritz Ebert on my behalf. He received the following reply ...

3.1.96

Lieber Herr Naugebauer!

Besten Dank für Ihren Brief vom 20. Dez. 1996.
In dem Lager Barony-Camp war ich von November 1944 -
März 1946. Dan kam ich in ein das Nebenlager Cargen
und war dort bis zu meiner Entlassung im Jan. 1948.
An den Namen kan ich mich nicht erinnern, es sind
auch schon 50 Jahre her.
In dem Brief schreiben Sie von der Kopie eines Bildes,
die Sie beilegen wollten. Ich habe aber nur die Kopie
der Engel gefunden. Wen Sie mir die Kopie des Bildes
schicken könnten könnte ich Ihnen genaueres berichten
Während des Krieges war bei den Gefangenen im Lager
schon gedrückte Stimmung weil sich die "Befreier" immer
mehr Deutschland näherten, in Deutschland eindrangen
und durch die Luftangriffe Städte und Dörfer zerstörten
Nach dem Kriegsende mußten wir bei Bauern oder im Wald arbei-
Da gab es dan mehr Abwechslung und man kam heraus aus
dem Stacheldraht. Das Leben war nicht mehr so eintönig.
Von den Engländern und der schottischen Bevölkerung wur-
wir korrekt und sehr gut behandelt. Sie sahen uns nicht
als Nazi~~soldaten~~verbrecher sondern als gute Soldaten an.
Vorher in den amerikanischen Gefangenenlagern in
Frankreich und England war die Behandlung und die
Verpflegung sehr schlecht weil dort deutsche Juden
als Lagerkomandanten waren.
Wen Sie noch weitere Fragen haben bin ich gerne bereit, diese
zu beantworten.
    Mit freundlichen Grüßen
                Fritz Ebert
            Landthurm 3
            74532 Ilshofen

So liegt Rentweinsdorf?

19

In English his letter reads as follows ... I stayed at Barony Camp from November 1944 until March 1946. Then I was taken to a smaller camp, Cargen, where I remained until I was dismissed in January 1948. I can't remember the name Alfred Bojanitz, it's fifty years ago. During the war prisoners lived in a depressed atmosphere because the 'deliveries' approached and entered Germany and destroyed cities and villages by air attacks. After the war we had to work on farms or in the forest. Such work meant we could leave the camp and things weren't so monotonous. The English and Scottish people treated us correctly and very well. We were not Nazi criminals but good soldiers in their eyes.

The time before this period, at American prison camps in France and England *it was very bad because the commanders of the camp were American Jews.

The report on compound D mentions the excellent choir. Below is a copy of a hand drawn birthday card depicting one of the nissen huts. The members of the mandolin concert band have signed the card for Franz Debeuser whose birthday falls on 28th October, 1948.

* The translation here is not literal as the phrase "German Jew" in Fritz Ebert's letter is a likely error. My father experienced similar treatment under an American Jew commander.

Perhaps that happy memory inspired Franz Debeuser to contact 'Barony camp' from his home in Robern Germany, many years later. In his correspondence he included an updated photo and a memento from his days spent at Barony Camp.

Arnold Becker decided to remain in England as this testimony indicates.

T E S T I M O N Y

POW No. A 828 721   Ogfr. BECKER, Arnold

The a/n has been employed with the Camp-Staff since 1944 and is only leaving for repatriation.

He proved most satisfactory and reliable in his service as Ration-Storeman in one of the Camp-Cookhouses.

I can recommend him for employment of this nature.

The Barony Camp,
nr. Dumfries,
Scotland.
11th Sept 1947.

INTERPRETER   S/Sgt.

298 GERMAN P.O.W. WORKING CAMP

The Grandson of Paul Leuschner wrote the following letter to a local newspaper in Scotland. I hope he was able to get in touch with the people of Dalscone.

FORMER POW SEEKS HELP

● **A letter written by a relative of a former German prisoner of war, has been passed on to us. The ex-POW, Mr Paul Leuschner, is seeking information about a farming family from whom he worked immediately after the War. The letter reads:**

Sir, — My name is Veiko Boden. I'm 26 years old and live in the German Democratic Republic.

I write to you by order of my grandfather. His name is Paul Leuschner and he is 80 years old.

My grandfather was stationed on the Channel Island Jersey during the last month of World War II. At the end of the war he was sent, together with other German men as a prisoner of war, to Dalscone near Dumfries.

There he stood from 1945 to December of 1947. He worked during these years at the farm of Mister Taylor. This farm was located near the links.

At the time, there were also employed Mister Ingles and Mister Ries. I enclose a photo. The photo (taken in September 1946) shows the two children of Mister Bob Ries.

My grandfather tells very often about his stay at your village; especially he likes to tell about the work at the farm. This farmer and also the farm labourer used my grandfather very good. He remembers with thankfulness of that time.

Now he lives together with his wife in a little village in the district of Cottbus in the German Democratic Republic.

He had to work very

● *The 1946 photograph showing the children of Bob Ries.*

hard all his life and all the time, since he returned from Britain to Germany.

He has given the promise to Mister Taylor to hold peace to the British people all his lifetime. And this promise he has kept. And in this sense he has also educated us, his grandsons.

He is very interested in learning something about the life of Mr Taylor, Mr Ries and Mr Ingles and the

daily Dalscone life. He would be pleased to get some information from you. Perhaps you can find out the acquaintance of my grandfather, or their sons and grandsons.

We would like to get in touch with them or other citizens of your region.

Veiko Boden,
in order of
Paul Leuscher,
Choriner Str. 9,
G.D.R. Berlin 1054.

Barony Camp Football Team 1947

Wilhelm Freise is in the second row (halfback). After returning to Germany he took up an important post as 'Professor fur Nordische Philologie' in Lubingen.

At Barony Camp: Fritz Ebert, second man from the right, was captured in Nancy, France in 1944. He was at Barony Camp until 1948.

Prisoner of War work party at Barony Camp.

Further photographic record of Prisoners of War at Barony.

In this group at Barony the first young man on the right of the back row was sent to Devon. He is also seen at the centre of the back row in the Chaddlewood (Plympton) work party below.

Alfred Bojanitz is second from right in the front row.

On the reverse of this photo that he sent to his Godson's parents in Neubeckum, Westfalia the following is recorded: Alfred Bojanitz A 95042 H Chaddlewood House no.137 q (?)Plympton. c/o G.P.O Devon. p.o.w.

Prisoners from Kitley worked in various areas. Plymstock, Wembury, Chaddlewood, Kingsbridge, Bigbury and Whitchurch are included in documents and recollections. The first document on the following pages show that my father worked on Mr. Osborne's farm at Kingsbridge. I am told my father walked from Kingsbridge to Hollacombe during exceptional blizzards one Christmas to see his sweetheart Edna. During my father's time at Kingsbridge Edna wrote a letter to a national newspaper and it was accepted and printed. In it she pointed out that prisoners of war who were meant to be doing farm work were illegally being 'sub contracted' for building roads and similar work.

Chaddlewood House in present times.

VERTRAG

Mr. F.M. Osborne,   Woodcombe, Chivelstone, Kingsbridge.
Zwischen dem _____(farmer)_____,wohnhaft _____(address),
(von nun ab "Landwirt" genannt) einerseits, und dem **Botjanitz**_____ (worker)
(von nun ab "Arbeiter" genannt) andererseits, wurde am **twelfth**
des Monats _____April____ 1948, das folgende vereinbart:-

1.   Der Landwirt wird den Arbeiter einstellen und der Arbeiter wird dem Landwirt
als landwirtschaftlicher Arbeiter auf dem Gut des Landwirts in **Chivelstone,**
dienen, unter und gemaess den folgenden Bedingungen und Grundsaetzen:-

2.   Die Beschaeftigungsdauer ist fuer die Zeit vom _____**twelfth**_____ Tage
des Monats _____**April**_____ 1948, bis zum 31. Tag des Monats Dezember 1948
festgelegt, falls sie nicht vorher dadurch beendigt wird, dass eine der beiden
Parteien der anderen eine Woche Kuendigung gibt.

3.   Waehrend der Beschaeftigungsdauer wird der Arbeiter:
        (a) nicht von irgend jemand anderem als dem Landwirt oder mit anderer als
            landwirtschaftlicher Arbeit beschaeftigt werden:

        (b) zu jeder Zeit die Pflichten eines Landarbeiters sorgfaeltig, so wie
            vom Landwirt verlangt, ausfuehren;

        (c) Dem Landwirt den Betrag von £1 - 6 fuer die Kosten der Bekleidung,
            welche von den Militaerbehoerden zusaetzlich der Bekleidung erlaubt
            worden ist, welche normalerweise von heimgesandten deutschen
            Kriegsgefangenen behalten werden kann, zurueckzahlen. Die Zurueckzahlung
            wird unter den Bedingungen stattfinden, die seitens der beiden Parteien
            zu Beginn des Arbeitsverhaeltniss arrangiert worden sind.
            Der Betrag wird von dem Landwirt an Stelle des Arbeiters den
            Militaerbehoerden bezahlt werden.

Der Landwirt wird:

        (a) Dem Arbeiter einen Lohn zahlen, welcher nicht weniger als den Minimal
            und Ueberstundensatz darstellt, der zur Zeit seitens des landwirtschaft-
            lichen Lohnsatz-Ausschusses festgelegt worden ist (dieser Minimalsatz
            betraegt zur Zeit fuer erwachsene Arbeiter fuer eine 48 Stunden-Woche,
            ___£4.10.0.____);

        (b) Als Teilzahlung der Lochnung und an Stelle von Bargeld den Arbeiter
            mit voller Kost und Logis versehen, deren Wert von Zeit zu Zeit durch
            einen Erlass des Landwirtschaftlichen Lohnsatz-Ausschusses festgelegt
            wird (dieser Wert betraegt augenblicklich £1.10.0. pro Woche);

        (c) Dem Arbeiter solche bezahlten Ferien gewaehren, zu denen
            landwirtschaftliche Arbeiter zur Zeit gesetzlich befugt sind;

        (d) Den grafschaftlichen Exekutiv-Ausschuss fuer Kriegs-Landwirtschaft
            sofort benachrichtigen, falls eine der beiden Parteien das
            Arbeitsverhaeltnis gekuendigt hat;

        (e) SOWIE DIESER VERTRAG UNTERZEICHNET WORDEN IST, DEN MILITAERBEHOERDEN
            £1 - 6 FUER BEKLEIDUNG BEZAHLEN, die dem Arbeiter zuzueglich
            der Bekleidung gegeben worden ist, die heimgeschickte Kriegsgefangene
            normalerweise behalten duerfen. Der Landwirt wird diesen Betrag von
            dem Arbeiter zurueckerhalten, gemaess den Bedingungen die mit dem
            Arbeiter gemaess dessen Verpflichtung unter Paragraph 3(c) dieses
            Vertrages, vereinbart worden sind.

4.   Der Erlass des landwirtschaftlichen Lohnsatz-Ausschusses vom 3. Juli 46,
bezueglich Arbeiter ohne landwirtschaftliche Erfahrung soll nicht auf diesen
Vertrag Anwendung finden.

                        _F.M. Osborne_____ Landwirt

                        _Bojranitz_____ Arbeiter

Zeuge fuer die Unterschrift der beiden Parteien:
Name: _H.C. Afton_____ Anschrift: ___1, The Plains, Totnes._

Beruf _____

        6d Briefmarke
                        den,
                                                                    Zeuge
                        twelfth Tag des Monats April 1948.

28

VERTRAG

Mr. E.L. Morrish,   Woodside, Gt. Churchways, Plymstock.
Zwischen dem   (farmer)   ,wohnhaft   (address),
(von nun ab "Landwirt" genannt) einerseits, und dem A. Bojanitz (worker)
(von nun ab "Arbeiter" genannt) andererseits, wurde am fourth
des Monats May 1948, das Folgende vereinbart:-

1.   Der Landwirt wird den Arbeiter einstellen und der Arbeiter wird dem Landwirt
als landwirtschaftlicher Arbeiter auf dem Gut des Landwirts in Plymstock
di enen, unter und gemaess den folgenden Bedingungen und Grundsaetzen:-

2.   Die Beschaeftigungsdauer ist fuer die Zeit von fourth Tage
des Monats May 1948, bis zum 31. Tag des Monats Dezember 1948
festgelegt, falls sie nicht vorher dadurch beendigt wird, dass eine der beiden
Parteien der anderen eine Woche Kuendigung gibt.

3.   Waehrend der Beschaeftigungsdauer wird der Arbeiter:
     (a) nicht von irgend jemand anderem als dem Landwirt oder mit anderer als
         landwirtschaftlicher Arbeit beschaeftigt werden:

     (b) zu jeder Zeit die Pflichten eines Landarbeiters sorgfaeltig, so wie
         vom Landwirt verlangt, ausfuehren;

     (c) Dem Landwirt den Betrag von £_____ fuer die Kosten der Bekleidung,
         welche von den Militaerbehoerden zusaetzlich der Bekleidung erlaubt
         worden ist, welche normalerweise von heimgesandten deutschen
         Kriegsgefangenen behalten werden kann, zurueckzahlen. Die Zurueckzahlung
         wird unter den Bedingungen stattfinden, die seitens der beiden Parteien
         zu Beginn des Arbeitsverhaeltniss arrangiert worden sind.
         Der Betrag wird vom Landwirt an Stelle des Arbeiters den
         Militaerbehoerden bezahlt werden.

Der Landwirt wird:

     (a) Dem Arbeiter einen Lohn zahlen, welcher nicht weniger als den Minimal
         und Ueberstundensatz darstellt, der zur Zeit seitens des landwirtschaft-
         lichen Lohnsatz-Ausschusses festgelegt worden ist (dieser Minimalsatz
         betraegt zur Zeit fuer erwachsene Arbeiter fuer eine 48 Stunden-Woche,
         £4.10.0.);

     (b) Als Teilzahlung der Loehnung und an Stelle von Bargeld den Arbeiter
         mit voller Kost und Logis versehen, deren Wert von Zeit zu Zeit durch
         einen Erlass des Landwirtschaftlichen Lohnsatz-Ausschusses festgelegt
         wird (dieser Wert betraegt augenblicklich £1.10.0. pro Woche);

     (c) Dem Arbeiter solche bezahlten Ferein gewaehren, zu denen
         landwirtschaftliche Arbeiter zur Zeit gesetzlich befugt sind;

     (d) Den grafschaftlichen Exekutiv-Ausschuss fuer Kriegs-Landwirtschaft
         sofort benachrichtigen, falls eine der beiden Parteien das
         Arbeitsverhaeltnis gekuendigt hat;

     (e) SOWIE DIESER VERTRAG UNTERZEICHNET WORDEN IST, DEN MILITAERBEHOERDEN
         £ FUER BEKLEIDUNG BEZAHLEN, die dem Arbeiter zuzeglich
         der Bekleidung gegeben worden ist, die heimgeschickte Kriegsgefangene
         normalerweise behalten duerfen. Der Landwirt wird diesen Betrag von
         dem Arbeiter zurueckerhalten, gemaess den Bedingungen die mit dem
         Arbeiter gemaess dessen Verpflichtung unter Paragraph 3(c) dieses
         Vertrages, vereinbart worden sind.

4.   Der Erlass des landwirtschaftlichen Lohnsatz-Ausschusses vom 3. Juli 46,
bezueglich Arbeiter ohne landwirtschaftliche Erfahrung soll nicht auf diesen
Vertrag Anwendung finden.

                           E.L. Morrish   Landwirt

                           Bojanitz A.   Arbeiter

Zeuge fuer die Unterschrift der beiden Parteien:
Name: *H.C. Holman*   Anschrift: 3, Union Street, Newton Abbot.

Beruf _____

      6d Briefmarke
             den.   Zeuge

29

Wembury Prisoner of War Workers

Heinrich Dennhoven

In 1987 Johannes Löscher read an article about Heinrich Dennhoven in a local newspaper. He contacted him and subsequently my parents received a postcard from Heinrich.

```
Lieber Kamerad Alfred und Familie !
Ich habe Dein " Lebenszeichen" mit viel Freude
und Dakbarkeit erhalten.Getrübt war diese Freude
allerdings durch den Umstand,daß ich leider seit
einigen Jahren nahezu völlig erblindet bin.Sonst
wäre es durchaus denkbar gewesen,Dich un die Deinen
bei Gelegenheit mal persömlich aufzusuchen.Das geht
nun leider nicht. Ich habe in den vergangenen Jahr=
zehnten oft und wieder an unsere Kameradschaft im
Lager und auf den Arbeitsplätzen in England gedacht.
Als ich nach Hause entlassen wurde fand ich nur
ein Trümmerfeld vor,das nur dem Namen nach noch
ein Dorf war.Wie Dir man die Ansichtskarte zeigt,
ist wieder ein neues, schönes Dorf aus den Trümmern
entstanden. Ffag allerdings nicht,was das an Knochen
Entbehrungen,Zeit und Geld gekostet hat.
        Und nun sehr herzliche Grüße und Wünsche vom
        Deinem Kameraden  Heinrich Dennhoven ,auch von
        Haus zu Haus.Lasse bald wieder etwas von Dir
                                              hören .
```

Translation:

Dear companion Alfred and Family,

I have received the 'lifesigns' from you with much joy and gratitude. 'However, this joy is somewhat marred by the fact that I have been totally blind for a few years now. Otherwise it would have been quite possible to visit you personally. Unfortunately it is not possible now. During the past decades I have again and again often thought about our friendship in the p.o.w camp and our places of work in England.

When I was allowed to return home, what I found there was just a field of ruins that was just a village in name only. As you can see from the picture (post card) a new and beautiful village has risen out of the ruins. Just don't ask me what it cost in hard work, in shortages, in rations and time and money. And now, the very warmest greetings and wishes from your friend Heinrich Dennhoven and from everyone here ... House Johruse.

Let us hear about yourself soon.

The news article Johannes Löscher noticed is shown opposite.

Translation of the article .....

Heinrich Dennhoven

Inden Pier: The 75 year old farmer Heinrich Dennhoven from Pier has been engaged in his profession for decades. His work in the public service in the professional organizations and also in local politics has been rewarded with a Federal Service cross. Landwirt (agronomist/farmer) Johannes Kaptain awarded him this distinguished decoration yesterday during a festive period at the Düren province (County Court). After a long period as a prisoner of war Heinrich Dennhoven returned to his totally destroyed home town of Pier in February 1948. In that same year he made himself available for setting up the Grazing Land Cooperative.

Farmer since 1957

In 1957 Heinrich Dennhoven became a farmer and the chairman of the local Farmers' Union'. He held these posts until 1981. In 1961 he was chosen a member of The Board of Directors' (in his capacity as District Farmer) of the sewage handling unit in Duren. In this functional role he represented, with much contribution, the interests and concerns of the union and its members. Farmer Kaptain thanked him for the part he played at that time, in building and paving the way for the future.

Besides eliminating the danger of free handling and removing sewage, the unit has also taken great trouble in creating agricultural fields out of the marshy fields in the Ruvane area.

Heinrich Dennhoven:

Für heimische Landwirtschaft viel geleistet

Inden-Pier. – Der 75jährige Landwirt Heinrich Dennhoven aus Pier hat sich jahrzehntelang engagiert für die Belange seines Berufsstandes eingesetzt. Seine ehrenamtliche Arbeit in den Berufsorganisationen und auch in der Kommunalpolitik wurden jetzt mit dem Bundesverdienstkreuz gewürdigt. Landrat Johannes Kaptain überreichte die hohe Auszeichnung gestern während einer Feierstunde im Dürener Kreishaus.

Nach langer Kriegsgefangenschaft kehrte Heinrich Dennhoven im Februar 1948 in seinen völlig zerstörten Heimatort Pier zurück. Noch im gleichen Jahr stellte er sich für die Arbeit in der Weidegenossenschaft Pier zur Verfügung und 1949 wurde er auch Vorstandsmitglied der Bullenhaltungsgenossenschaft.

Seit 1957 Ortslandwirt

1957 wurde Heinrich Dennhoven zum Ortslandwirt und Vorsitzenden der Ortsbauernschaft bestellt. Diese Ämter übte er bis 1981 aus. Im Jahre 1961 wurde er in seiner Eigenschaft als Ortslandwirt von der Verbandsversammlung des Abwasserbehandlungsverbandes Düren in den Vorstand gewählt. In dieser Funktion hat er über 20 Jahre lang die Interessen des Verbandes und dessen Mitglieder mit großem Einsatz vertreten. Landwirt Kaptain dankte dem Landwirt dafür, daß er wesentlich dazu beigetragen habe, eine für die damalige Zeit wegweisende Einrichtung mitaufzubauen.

Neben der gefahrlosen Beseitigung des Abwassers habe sich der Verband mit großem Erfolg um die Schaffung landwirtschaftlicher Flächen in der Ruraue bemüht.

Im Gemeinderat

Weitere Verdienste hat sich Heinrich Dennhoven durch seine Tätigkeit im Rat der seinerzeit selbständigen Gemeinde Pier erworben. Von 1961 bis 1969 – also in der entscheidenden Phase vor der kommunalen Neugliederung – war er als Kommunalpolitiker tätig.

Der Indener Bürgermeister Willi Wolff bescheinigte Heinrich Dennhoven, daß sein Herz ein Leben lang für die Landwirtschaft und die Belange seiner Berufskollegen geschlagen habe.   -de-

Heinrich Denhoven aus Pier hat sich in landwirtschaftlichen Berufsorganisationen Verdienste erworben.   Foto: Dietmar Engels

At the Council

Heinrich Dennhoven achieved further merits through his activity in the Pier Town Council which, in his time, was an independent unit. from 1961 to 1969, i.e in the decisive phase prior to community reorganization he was active as a local politician. The Mayor of the town of Inden, Willie Wolff testified on behalf of Heinrich that "His heart had beaten only for agriculture and the professional field of his colleagues throughout his working life".

Heinrich Dennhoven from Pier has obtained merits/decorations for work with agricultural guilds and organizations.

In 2001 I was in touch with Katharina Dennhoven and her daughter Salome Bünger who kindly lent me some photographs.

Left: Heinrich, his wife Katharina and their son Peter who was born in 1943.

Right: Heinrich during retirement years.

The Dennhoven family standing inside their bombed farm building.

With the assistance of helpers Katharina restored the building. This symbol of hope awaited Heinrich when he returned from England in 1948.

The recollections of Maria Salome Bünger .....

My father Heinrich was born on 30th June 1909. He married my mother Katharina on 27th August 1941. He died on 25th July 1988. He was one of eight children and was brought up by his Aunt and Uncle. They owned a farm that he later inherited.

My brother Heinz Peter was born in 1943 and I was born in 1945. I have

Heinrich relaxing at home with his dog.

two daughters Sandra and Tanja. When my father returned from captivity in 1948 I didn't know who he was. Our village lay in ash and rubble after the war. Before my father returned my mother rebuilt the cow shed with the assistance of helpers. From 1948 until 1953 my parents built up the farm including a new house and in 1953 we moved into the new house.

My father always thought back on his time in England. He always dreamed of England a great deal. My brother continues in the footsteps of my father in his work at the County Court. My hometown Pier continues to have its brown coal excavated but this will expire after ten or fifteen years.

Heinrich, Katharina and granddaughters Sandra (born May 1974) and Tanja (born May 1977).

35

Johannes Löscher

In 1987 Johannes Löscher and his wife Elizabeth came over to England, from East Germany, to visit my parents.

Left to right: Alfred Bojanitz, Johannes and Elizabeth Löscher, Edna Bojanitz.

In 1987 the amalgamation of east and West Germany was barely in process. It was very difficult for Johannes and Elizabeth to obtain travel permits and passports. As a further deterrent they were not permitted to take any money with them.

In good faith (and a predicament reminiscent of war time) they set off with only their pre-paid coach ticket for London to Plymouth with them. The delay in the post had caused further havoc and their tickets arrived just in the nick of time.

The reunion was emotional for it never had never been possible whilst the Berlin Wall had stood. On the occasions I took them to various locations in my car Johannes, his wife and my parents eagerly discussed their shared memories.

"Ah yes, Whitchurch, that's where Heinrich worked for a time ... and Bigbury ... yes I was there" commented Johannes. At Bigbury during their holiday Johannes met a farm worker who remembered him. They laughed as they recalled how the farmer and his family had included Johannes in the weekly visit to the local pub, even though it was against the rules. The family had clothed him so that he looked 'a typical but noticeably quiet English lad'. My mother commented "I guess they got up to all kinds of pranks. Besides Johannes was only in his twenties".

After Johannes and Elizabeth had returned to Germany I asked my mother to write down her recollections of the time she worked at Old Barton.

Edna's recollections .....

I first met Johannes Löscher in 1945. He was one of five Prisoners of War who came to work on the farm. Their first task was to hoe out mangolds in a field above the farm house. My first sight of the prisoners was of them on the skyline working in the field. It made a lasting impression on my artistic mind. Whether it was intentional or not, Karl, who was tallest, took the lead. Then came 'Booby' who was only eighteen (thus the nick-name). Next in line was Heinrich who was like a real father to the others. Aged about thirty-five, he was a farmer in its true sense and had many skills. Johannes Löscher followed and last in line was 'little Alfred', the smallest of them all.

At the end of the month Johannes and Heinrich were selected to stay on at the farm to work for a further period of time. We two land girls had to make ourselves scarce because, officially, English girls were not allowed to work with Prisoners of War.

Johannes' recollections .....

In 1994, a year after my mother's death, I wrote to Johannes Löscher and asked him about his memories. His reply was as follows ...

Early in the summer of 1945 we came to Kitley Hostel at Brixton. From there we went to work on farms and some other places. The five of us were sent to 'The Old Barton Farm' to the family Lugar. Your Dad and me and Heinrich and two other men. Your Mum worked on the farm. In the Autumn Mr. Lugar needed only two men for milking the cows, and Heinrich and I remained on the farm. Before Christmas we lived on the farm. Jimmy Lugar was very ill and had to go to hospital. We had plenty of work to do.

Of a Sunday we could go to the village. Sometimes I went to the church. The people were always nice. We came to know some people. Near the farm was the vicarage where Mr. Tagg, the vicar, lived. In the village lived an old man called Jo, who lived at the house called Marconi. Every question you asked ... you got an answer from him!

Bob Philips was the cobbler. Two men lived in the house called Escalonia. The name of one was Oliver, the other I have forgotten. In the big house down the bottom, lived a woman who worked for the household. Her name was Udell. In the Manor House near the farm worked a butler. He had a very old car which he could turn at the end of the road.

At the beginning of 1947 there were heavy snows and many roads were closed. We left the farm in 1947 owing to some trouble. Heinrich then went to Whitchurch to work and I went to Saltram Park in Chaddlewood. I also worked at Bigbury on Sea.

At the end of 1947 I went home.

Maria's Postcript

I would like to add ... Bob Philips later ran South Barton Farm at Brownhill Lane. In those days the farm covered a larger area. My mother worked there for a number of years in the nineteen sixties. I remember going with her to herd in the cows from the fields where the houses of Hawthorn Drive and Veasy Park now stand. Bob's family have continued to run the farm after him.

The house called Marconi that Johannes remembered is the present day vicarage in Church Road. During the 1940's and 1950's it was owned by Mr. and Mrs. Joliff of Cross Park Road. The house where the lady called Udell worked and lived is Thorn House near the River Yealm. The manor house is Wembury House. The butler was Mr. Henshaw. Jimmy Lugar, mentioned by Johannes, was a boy at that time. He explained he nearly died of double pneumonia during the time Johannes referred to.

Left: Reverend Tagg, Rogation Sunday 1948

Below: A present day photograph of the former vicarage

Rogationtide Service 1948,
conducted by Reverend Tagg

St. Werburgh's Church 1948 ... Rogation Sunday.

"The people were very nice" (Johannes Löscher).

Left to right the people are: Mr. Russell Snell, Reverend Tagg, Jennifer Clifton (child), Peter Eames (child), Mrs. Thomson, Mrs. Erscott, Jimmy Lugar (child), Joyce Russell (young lady), Ruth Dawe (child), Peter Lugar (child), Mrs. Elthel Burrows, Christine Clifton (child), Mrs. Densum, Mr. Ben Clifton, Creber family, Mrs. Doris Wills, Mr. Herbert Wills, Pat Snell (babe), Pat Sargeant, Barbara Snell (child), Mrs. Eva Snell.

My Journey

In May 1997 I visited Johannes and Elizabeth Löscher in Schwarzenberg, East Germany. At the time of my visit Johannes' health was deteriorating as he had been on kidney dialysis some eight years. My father's Godson, Alfred Neugebauer, kindly drove me to Schwarzenberg from his family home in Saxony. Later the same day Alfred drove back to his family whilst I stayed with the Johannes and Elizabeth a few days.

'' Your mother was a very good woman" said Johannes as he recalled her fair-mindedness and kindness to the five Prisoners of War. As he spoke the words 'In Christ there is no East or West' came to my mind.

I enjoyed seeing various places in Schwarzenberg. The wooded hills and castle reminded me of German folk tales. The little shops were full of hand crafted items such as 'nut cracker men', hand made lace and carvings of woodland scenes and deer.

We were able to walk a few yards across the border to a market in Czechoslovakia. The police checking the passports looked politely baffled when they saw my surname on an English passport.

The few days passed quickly and on the last day Johannes hired a taxi. He accompanied me the fifty miles or so to the nearest railway station. He explained that the taxi driver drove him to the hospital every other day for dialysis and that over the years they had become friends. It was fortunate for me to be so well looked after in a strange country.

As I was about to get on the train at the railway station Johannes placed an envelope in my hand. "That's for the train journey" he said and wouldn't take it back. Not until I exchanged the money back in England did I realize their gift covered not only the train fare but much of the air fare as well. I realized, with tears in my eyes and heart, this was their way of expressing their appreciation of the friendship of special origin they had shared with my parents. In his letters over the years Johannes often had reflected upon Edna's unbiased kindness towards the Prisoners of War.

The taxi driver and Johannes (right) at the railway station some miles from Schwarzenberg.

Post Script ... I was in touch with Elizabeth Löscher in the Autumn of 1997 when Johannes' health deteriorated considerably. One day Elizabeth telephoned to let me know that Johannes had died. He is not forgotten by his German and English friends. I am glad I went to Schwarzenberg in May 1997, a journey my parents had hoped to make.

Schwarzenberg 1997
A view of the town with the pinnacles of the castle way above the trees.

Elizabeth and Johannes   Maria (me) and Elizabeth

Mr. Kenneth O'Connor recalls .....

Kenneth's recollections possibly piece together the mystery of the fifth prisoner of war. Was he Kurt Hollman? He recalls that Kurt came from Czechoslovakia as a refugee. He believes he came here before the war and that he may have have been Jewish. The fact that Kurt worked for the Slades at Old Barton Farm ties in with the pre war time zone. Kenneth recalls that Kurt often went to the 'Jubilee Inn' at ten, after a hard day's work.

This pattern indicates he might have come to England before full scale war developed and that during the war he would have been some eighteen years of age.

Perhaps he was among the many children and young people who were rescued from Czechoslovakia and brought to England. Could this have been the reason my mother remembered a lad of eighteen? But to add to the mystery Mr Godfrey Smallridge insists the fifth prisoner of war in the photo in question is not Kurt Hollman.

Kenneth recalls with amusement how Kurt attempted to join 'The Home Guard'. This indicates he was not a Prisoner of War but regardless of the fact his application was rejected. Perhaps this is why he identified with the Prisoners of War. I mentioned to Kenneth how easy it was for me to walk to a market in Czechoslovakia from Schwarzenberg in East Germany. He agreed that the close proximity of East Germany to Czechoslovakia may have provided Kurt with geographical identification with Prisoners of war. It is feasible that Kurt would have identified with the East German prisoner, Johannes Löscher and with Alfred Bojanitz who had been ousted out of Jugoslavia before full scale war had developed.

Kenneth's recollections stretch back before the war. He remembers a wind-up petrol pump at the present day location of Knighton Store. Petrol was elevenpence ha'penny a gallon. Due to rationing and economic pressures the petrol station had to be closed down. During the war all pumps had to have glass cylinders so that the petrol flow was clearly visible.

Kenneth also remembers happy times with his friend George Body. The lads often visited Langdon Woods. Frequently they had to scarper as Mr Erscott the gamekeeper patrolled the woods. Undoubtedly such respectable young men would never have poached rabbits! On one occasion they witnessed a host of Spitfires returning from France.

Mr. Kenneth O'Connor in his Home Guard uniform in 1941. He is the proud owner of the 1939 Morris Minor.

Kenneth remembers his colleagues in the Home Guard .....

Mr. Woodley, Mr. Henry Lugar, Mr. Basil Humphrey, Mr. Ian Mc Claran, Mr. Ian Perring, Sergeant Weeks, Captain Giles, Mr. Vincent. Mr. Sam Little, Mr. Alfie Newmann, Mr. Wolfe, Mr. Henshaw. Mr. Woodley lived in the game-keeper's cottage near Hollacombe. Sergeant Weeks was another Hollacombe man. Mr. Henry Lugar was the farmer at Old Barton Farm. Mr. Perring lived at 'The Jubilee Inn'. His colleague Ian McClaren, who liked to join him for a game of darts, always scored highest at the Ivybridge rifle range in his Home Guard days. Captain Giles and his wife were familiar figures in Wembury during the 1950's and 1960's and were regular church members. During that period they lived at New Barton Farm. Mr. Alfie Newmann was brother of Dolly Newmann (Mrs. Carn) of Knighton Road. As children they attended Wembury Primary School in Ford Road. During the 1940's Mr. Wolfe owned Wembury Stores and ran a local taxi service. He emigrated to New Zealand.

In 1940, due to intense bombing in London, the Eagle Oil Shipping Company operated at Langdon Court. Mrs. Kekwick was secretary for the company. Later she moved to Wembury. Owing to the escalation of bombing the army next took over Langdon Court. In the final stages of the war, and for a short time afterwards Langdon Court was used as a childrens' hospital and had residential nurses.

Kenneth and his wife Gwenda (1999)

Julian Hodges, the son of the director of the Eagle Star Shipping Company, at West Wembury Farm where his family lodged.

George Body in a bomb crater at Mountpleasant Farm. Perhaps his thoughts are of the close proximity to Langdon Court.

George Body driving a tractor of the 1940's.
Kurt is likely to have driven a similar tractor at Old Barton Farm.

The Girls of the Corporation Office

Prior to working at Old Barton Farm Edna worked in Pophams and then at The Plymouth Corporation Office.

Edna is first left behind the four young ladies in the fore of the photograph. Her friend Hilda Harlow (1st right of the same row) married Norman Mitchell, one of the original gunners at H.M.S Cambridge, Wembury Point.

During the war Hilda was missing several days. She had been the victim of a bombing raid near Plymouth Hoe. She needed extensive surgery as she had lost part of her jaw. Since that day she has had to live with a piece of shrapnel lodged in her neck, inoperable due its close proximity to the spinal cord.

The wedding day of Hilda and Norman Mitchell on 27th February 1943.
Edna is one of the bridesmaids (first left).

Marine band at the final open day at HMS Cambridge in 2000. HMS Cambridge
gunnery school closed on 30th March 2001. The decommissioning of the HMS
chapel of St. Barbara took place on Sunday 11th March 2001.

Kurt Hollman

There is a bit of a mystery surrounding the Prisoner of War called Kurt. Was the fifth man in the photograph of the Prisoners of War at Old Barton Farm a refugee called Kurt Hollman? Or was he another man with the same Christian name?

The death certificate of Kurt Hollman ties in with recollections of a terrible tractor accident in the memories of those who worked on the farm at that time. It would seem unlikely that two accidents would have occurred at the same spot in the same period of history.

What is known, is that the Kurt who worked with the Prisoners of War at Old Barton Farm identified with them. Recollections place the accident during the war but we need to remember that 1951 (the date of death on the certificate) was one of the transition years into peace time.

Edna wrote a letter to Kurt's sister (an American citizen) to let her know the tragic news. Already she had corresponded during the war to indirectly let her know her brother had survived. It seems odd that he was unable to correspond himself. Might that have been to do with refugee or Prisoner of War status? Edna gave it the latter emphasis. Whatever the reason, Kurt, as a person of dual nationality, felt vulnerable.

The x on this early postcard indicates the spot where (as my mother recalled) Kurt had his fatal accident. The death certificate affirms the location.

The death certificate (registration district in the sub district of Yealmpton) of Kurt Hollman of Marconi House, Church Road, Wembury, provides the following information:

Kurt died on 11th April 1951 in a field on Old Barton Farm. He was aged twenty-eight. On 15th April an inquest was held. The coroner's report was that the death was accidental and that he died of severe crush injuries of the abdomen and chest causing asphyxia, received by his being crushed by the wheel of an overturned tractor against the wall.

Is this man in the centre Kurt Hollman ?

Alfred Bojanitz

My father Alfred was born in Neubeckum near Münster in Westfalia, Germany in 1917. His mother Marija was Austro Hungarian and came from Futog, a town that in its history had been part of Serbia but that had been taken over by the Austro-Hungarian Empire. His father Elias was Jugoslav and came from Besereck near Belgrade. Elias, Marija and their children had left Jugoslavia, a year or two before the First World War broke. Elias had to fight for Germany in Russia.

Marija's untimely death happened when Alfred was ten years old. A year or so later Elias returned to Belgrade with his children, three of whom were German born citizens.

Elias and Marija Bojanitz with their daughter Kate (circa 1912), in Jugoslavia.

By the time the Second World War broke out in 1939, Alfred was twenty-two. Having recently been a novice monk he was helping a priest with mission work in Belgrade. The Priest, Augustus Hegenkötter came from Alfred's home town, Neubeckum and his work involved reuniting members of displaced German families. Alfred often assisted in the evenings when films, with a religious theme, were shown to keep youths off the streets. Once war had been declared much racial hatred against German citizens escalated in Jugoslavia. A number of innocent people were arrested and interrogated. Whilst doing his mission work Alfred was arrested and taken to a police cell for day and night where he was interrogated and beaten with rubber truncheons. Perhaps by law people were only kept for twenty-four hours. The following morning Alfred was left for dead on the street and all the money he possessed had been stolen. Thankfully he was rescued by Augustus Hegenkötter.

When Alfred had sufficiently recovered Augustus helped him escape to Germany. This was achieved by crawling through the end of a private garden under the cover of darkness and embarking a train. Equipped with a convincing passport that Augustus arranged, he hid for most of the journey. One can speculate that by the same method this priest and the people who lived in the house with the garden backing onto the railway line junction helped saved the lives of Germans. It seems certain many would have been killed illegally had they remained in Jugoslavia. In Germany all men of working age were conscripted into the 'Wehrmacht'.

Alfred received cadet training at the town of Aachen, some fifty miles from Cologne near the Belgium border. His training in horsemanship in the Vienna Riding School in Lubljana and his ability to speak Jugoslav and a little Russian were taken into consideration by the authorities before they decided to send him to Aachen.

Some time later when he was on leave an English bomb, aimed at St. Joseph's Church fell some yards from the target. Sadly the bomb landed on an air raid shelter where a water main was ruptured. Before they could be reached, the occupants, including Alfred's fiance, were drowned inside the bomb shelter.

The cadets at Aachen: Alfred is 2nd from right in the front row.

Epitaph: Helmut Woste (Helmut is first left in the front row of the Aachen cadets).

Oft hast Du an uns geschrieben,
Sorgen macht Euch nicht, Ihr Lieben,
Im Himmel gibt's ein Wiederseh'n.
Auf Erden kann es nicht gescheh'n.
Weit ist Dein Grab, tief unser Schmerz,
Nun ruhe sanft, Du treues Herz.

Translation of poem:

Often you wrote to us

"Do not worry, my dear ones"

In Heaven we shall meet again.

On earth it cannot be.

Deep is your grave.

Great our pain.

Now rest in peace dear heart.

When Helmut was killed by Russian fire Alfred was standing next to him. Had Alfred been taller he also would have been killed. Alfred never forgot his friend.

"Whoso faithfully fought till the last bullet hit, and whoso thus dies, will not be forgotten.

In reverent remembrance of one who fell for the fatherland.

Helmut Woste, Lance Corporal in the Grenadier regiment

Great Germany. Bearer of the medal of the wounded who fell for the fatherland.

The dear fallen one was born on 23rd July 1924 in Langeberg and died the hero's death in soldierly duty and willing endeavour on 20th February 1944 near Kobowska. His grave is at the Heroes Cemetery Rownoje. He was able to spend Christmas with his dear ones and took leave for ever in January, 1944. This loss is even more greatly felt as a brother-in-law is missing at Stalingrad. The grieving parents and siblings lose with him a promising son and brother, the fiance her unforgettable bridegroom. God grant him for his sacrifice eternal life.

May he rest in God's holy peace!

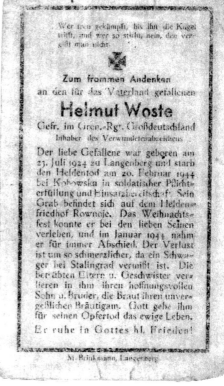

Wer treu gekämpft, bis ihn die Kugel
trifft, und wer so stirbt, nein, den ver-
gißt man nicht.

Zum frommen Andenken
an den für das Vaterland gefallenen

Helmut Woste

Gefr. im Gren.-Rgt. Großdeutschland
Inhaber des Verwundetenabzeichens

Der liebe Gefallene war geboren am
23. Juli 1924 zu Langenberg und starb
den Heldentod am 20. Februar 1944
bei Kobowska in soldatischer Pflicht-
erfüllung und Einsatzbereitschaft. Sein
Grab befindet sich auf dem Helden-
friedhof Rownoje. Das Weihnachts-
fest konnte er bei den lieben Seinen
verleben, und im Januar 1944 nahm
er für immer Abschied. Der Verlust
ist um so schmerzlicher, da ein Schwa-
ger bei Stalingrad vermißt ist. Die
betrübten Eltern u. Geschwister ver-
lieren in ihm ihren hoffnungsvollen
Sohn u. Bruder, die Braut ihren unver-
geßlichen Bräutigam. Gott gebe ihm
für seinen Opfertod das ewige Leben.

Er ruhe in Gottes hl. Frieden!

M. Brinkmann, Langenberg

Next, Alfred was sent to Smolensk in Russia where many men froze to death and others, including Alfred, suffered frost bite. One day a Russian threw a live grenade. It landed near Alfred's battalion and he ran and picked it up and threw it to a clear area. He saved his whole battalion and was awarded a medal* for this act of bravery. Alfred was a man of conscience and his private purpose was only to save life. On another occasion he was court martialled for another act of bravery. Ignoring rules and regulations he threw a loaf of bread to some starving Russian peasants from the train on which he was travelling. Someone reported him and for Alfred that was the start of being out of favour with his superiors. Whilst in Russia Alfred caught typhus fever and ended up at a Red Cross centre. After some days had passed he was believed to be dead and was put on a cart and taken to the makeshift mortuary. Thankfully he 'rose again' and lived to tell the tale.

Because of his mixed nationality Alfred suffered a great deal in the hands of those intent upon establishing what they perceived to be a 'pure race'. Along with millions of Jewish people, thousands of German people, particularly the handicapped, mentally ill, those of undefined nationality, anyone who didn't fit into the scheme of things, were gassed in the gas chambers and their bodies disposed of in incinerators along with the bodies of Jewish people. On several occasions my father narrowly escaped death under this 'system'. It seems sad that these victims are mainly forgotten. One prays they will be remembered as the truths of history are admitted and revealed. These forgotten German people were victims of the terrible holocaust.

Ordinary people were caught up in the events of war. When I visited Germany in 1997, I learned from the uncle of my father's Godson how he was made to enlist at gun point as he herded his milk cows along the road. "One minute I was seeing to the farm. The next minute someone in uniform roared up on a motorbike and a gun was placed at my temple".

As we learned earlier, my father was eventually captured on the edge of the Black Forest and taken to a Prisoner of War centre at Cherbourg in France from where he was taken to Southampton. From there he went to Dumfries and was then transferred to Brixton near Plymouth. At the end of the war when my father Alfred was at Kitley Prisoner of War Camp he was given work to do. He worked in the grounds and buildings of Chaddlewood House and on farms at Kingsbridge, Plymstock and on Old Barton Farm, Wembury, where he met my mother Edna. Despite language barriers Edna and Alfred knew they were destined for each other. It was love at first sight.

As they worked along side each other in the fields the Germans and English land girls exchanged language. They must have had a few laughs as a potato became a 'kartoffel' and a knife became a 'messer'. From that beginning the channels of communication opened up. Friend became 'freund' and love became 'liebe'.

Edna and Alfred began to understand each other's life story. They had a lot in common. They both had a strong Christian faith. When they were children they both had lost their mothers. They both had lost a brother (Johannes Bojanitz died in action in Morocco whilst serving in the French Foreign Legion some time before the Second World War). On the day Alfred was to leave Old Barton Farm he waved his hands at Edna and in desperation said "You be my wife?". Whilst Edna realized

* My mother told me this award was the 'Iron Cross'.

Alfred's communication difficulties she didn't give an answer at that early stage. After his work at Old Barton Farm had ended, Alfred couldn't forget Edna and corresponded via 'postman' Heinrich Dennhoven who remained on the farm a few months longer. Often a letter was hidden inside a loaf of bread and romance blossomed. In one of the letters Alfred expresses his concern about their meeting in a field near Kitley Camp.

"... It is very dangerous for us both. Did you read that news article about a German Prisoner of War and an English girl in the Land Army?"

In another letter he talks of weeping as he leaves Edna's home at Hollacombe because her father refuses his request to visit. He also has the courage to say he understands how her father must feel. George Henry was grieving the loss of his son earlier in the war.

My Grandfather, George Henry Sly, also bore in mind his own trials during the First World War. As a chief shipwright in the Royal Navy, he had received various medals for bravery. Such bravery had included that of saving his Captain when a section of the submarine they were on was shelled and flooded. George Henry wedged himself in the doorway that was closing off automatically, to seal off the flooded section, and pulled the Captain free. During my childhood my Grandfather sometimes related how the Captain had lost part of his foot during this ordeal. I used to question Grandad about his missing finger tips. He sometimes implied they may have been lost on that occasion but he never actually confirmed it. It is a well known fact that shipwrights in training sometimes received such injuries.

The helpful priest - Augustus Hegenkötter.

Translated material: Augustus Hegenkötter, born 3rd May 1885 in Neubeckum, went as a missionary to Jugoslavia and returned to Neubeckum in 1940 until 1962 when he became priest in Twistenden. He was particularly involved in researching the history of the Parish of St. Joseph. The picture is as chaplain.

Alfred as a soldier: He was privately traumatized by all the death and destruction he witnessed.

George Henry Sly R.N.
(This photo is likely to have been taken circa 1906).

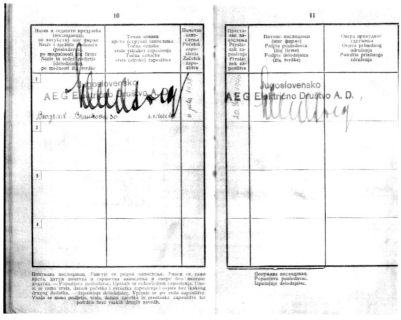

The following pages from Alfred's Jugoslav passport cause one to ask some questions:

1. Was the employers stamp and signature on page 10 a legal requirement? It most certainly would not be required during peace time. It appears to tie in with the authority stamp on page 6.

2. Does the employers stamp and signature on page 11 indicate that pages 10 and 11 were stamped at the same time for the purpose of making the passport appear authentic in the event of Alfred being located on the train?

3. There is no authority stamp on page 7. Does this mean Alfred disembarked unnoticed of his own accord en route? Does it mean he was able to give verbal explanation when he went through an authentic German check out point?

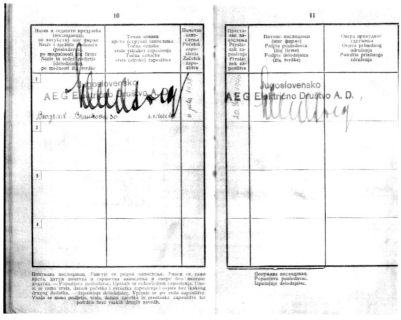

Edna cheered Alfred up by including her own cartoons in her letters.

Little Alfred gains height ....

... he's GREAT anyway.

Methode Gaspey-Otto-Sauer.

Kleine
Englische Sprachlehre

für

Schul-, Privat- und Selbstunterricht

von

Dr. Emil Otto.

Vollständig neubearbeitet

von

Professor Dr. S. J. Curtis,
Frankfurt a. M.

The Camp had a German-English dictionary. It must have come in very handy for love letters.

C E R T I F I C A T E.

BOJANITZ, Alfred - A 965042 -

The a/m is authorized to ride a pedal cycle

Type: STANDARD   No. V - 44431

within an area of 5 miles from the Kitley Hostel.

30th June 1947
Chaddlewood House
c/o GPO.   JOHN L. WEBBER   Capt. I.O.
Plympton, Devon.   for Commandant 137 German PW. Wkg. Camp.

Visiting a sweetheart was upgraded when the above document was issued ...

Edna

Alfred

French Foreign
Legion group:
one of the men
is Johannes
Bojanitz.

Alfred's sister Matilda remained
in Jugoslavia.

Alfred's sister Elizabeth, who fled
Jugoslavia with her fiance and
later married in England.

Elizabeth's husband Milorad Stefanovich, who fled Jugoslavia after his brother was shot dead for his non-communist beliefs. Elizabeth and Milorad settled in Canada and America.

1950: Milorad, Elizabeth, George Henry Sly holding Maria, Edna Bojanitz

Alfred Neugebauer back right and his wife Rachilda and their children.

His brother Berni Hanswille on the left at the back with his wife Gieslla in front of him.

After the war ......

After the war becoming an English citizen was no easy process. Former Prisoners of War had to return to Germany as part of the "Operation Repat" programme. Food ration book, clothing coupon book and National Registration identity card had to be submitted before the start of the journey. Only then were travel warrants issued. Alfred had to travel by train to London. Once there he found the connection for Liverpool Street Station from where he travelled third class to Parkstone Quay in Harwich. Classified as aliens, ex Prisoners of War were subsequently issued with a Police Certificate of registration as an alien. This certificate was stamped at the outset and at the end of the return journey. At Harwich the men had to make a compulsory deposit of £1.00. They were issued with receipts so that they could collect their deposit once they had returned from Germany. They were accommodated for one night at a transit camp at Parkstone Quay where they received a free evening meal and breakfast.

In the morning they were taken to Parkstone Quay to board a ship that took them to the Hook of Holland. As they were not allowed to take any money with them food and drink was supplied during the voyage. At the Hook of Holland they were taken to a dispersal centre at Münster, Westfalia.

In Münster former Prisoners of War were given a discharge certificate that entitled them to food and free travel to their destination. At their home address they received ration cards from the Burgemeister for the period of their stay. Should an emergency have arisen they also carried United Kingdom credit certificates and could receive payment at certain centres. Unclaimed credits could also be cashed upon return to England. Ex-Prisoners of War had to return to England with an appropriate discharge certificate and medical certificate. Having set out on December 15th, 1948, Alfred returned to England on January 13th, 1949.

Whilst he was in Westfalia he caught with a great deal of news and heard from Augustus Hegenkötter. Priests such as Augustus upheld the most holy bravery of Bishop August, Count von Galen, who, during 1941 preached sermons in defiance of the Nazis. His 'prophetic parable' was how the anvil would survive long after the hammer had worn out. He openly condemned the Nazi seizure of the abbeys and their acts of throwing religious orders into the streets. Alfred must have thought of his former religious community in Jugoslavia. Sadly, during the war the monks were murdered by communists. Bishop August, Count von Galen, condemned the Nazi usury and their cruelty to all German citizens. He relentlessly upheld the faith by condemning the Nazi complete denial of Christian love, compassion, morality and ethics. Because of his work Bishop August, Count von Galen was made a Cardinal.

Bishop von Galen of Münster

Footnote: Bishop von Galen's sermons and a brief summary of his life are available in booklet form from St. Lambert's Church in Münster.

CONTROL FORM D.2
Kontrollblatt D.2

CERTIFICATE OF DISCHARGE
Entlassungschein

ALL ENTRIES WILL BE MADE IN BLOCK LATIN CAPITALS AND WILL BE MADE IN INK OR TYPE-SCRIPT.	**I** **PERSONAL PARTICULARS** Personalbeschreibung	Dieses Blatt **muss** in folgender weise ausgefüllt werden: 1. In lateinischer Druckschrift und in grossen Buchstaben. 2. Mit Tinte oder mit Schreibmaschine.

SURNAME OF HOLDER ... *BOJANITZ*
Familienname des Inhabers

CHRISTIAN NAMES ... *ALFRED*
Vornamen des Inhabers

CIVIL OCCUPATION ... *KELLNER*
Beruf oder Beschäftigung

HOME ADDRESS Strasse ... *SWIED - 43*
Heimatanschrift   Ort ... *NIE WBECKUM*
Kreis ... *BECKUM*
Regierungsbezirk/Land
... *IM WIENSTIER*

DATE OF BIRTH ... *1.8.17*
Geburtsdatum (DAY/MONTH/YEAR
                                  Tag/Monat/Jahr)

PLACE OF BIRTH ... *NEUBECKUM*
Geburtsort

FAMILY STATUS SINGLE   † Ledig
Familienstand   MARRIED   Verheiratet /
                         WIDOW(ER) Verwitwet
                         DIVORCED   Geschieden

NUMBER OF CHILDREN WHO ARE MINORS
Zahl der minderjährigen Kinder ...

I HEREBY CERTIFY THAT TO THE BEST OF MY KNOWLEDGE AND BELIEF THE PARTICULARS GIVEN ABOVE ARE TRUE.
I ALSO CERTIFY THAT I HAVE READ AND UNDERSTOOD THE "INSTRUCTIONS TO PERSONNEL ON DISCHARGE" (CONTROL FORM D.1).
SIGNATURE OF HOLDER ... † *Bojanitz Alfred*
Unterschrift des Inhabers

Ich erkläre hiermit, nach bestem Wissen und Gewissen, dass die obigen Angaben wahr sind.
Ich bestätige ausserdem dass ich die "Anweisung für Soldaten und Angehörige Militär-ähnlicher Organisationen" u.s.w. (Kontrollblatt D.1) gelesen und verstanden habe.

II
MEDICAL CERTIFICATE
Ärztlicher Befund

DISTINGUISHING MARKS ...
Besondere Kennzeichen

DISABILITY, WITH DESCRIPTION
Dienstunfähigkeit, mit Beschreibung   *- / / -*

MEDICAL CATEGORY ...
Tauglichkeitsgrad

I CERTIFY THAT TO THE BEST OF MY KNOWLEDGE AND BELIEF THE ABOVE PARTICULARS RELATING TO THE HOLDER ARE TRUE AND THAT HE IS NOT VERMINOUS OR SUFFERING FROM ANY INFECTIOUS OR CONTAGIOUS DISEASE.

Ich erkläre hiermit, nach bestem Wissen und Gewissen, dass die obigen Angaben wahr sind, dass der Inhaber ungezieferfrei ist und dass er keinerlei ansteckende oder übertragbar Krankheit hat.

SIGNATURE OF MEDICAL OFFICER ...
Unterschrift des Sanitätsoffiziers

NAME AND RANK OF MEDICAL OFFICER IN BLOCK LATIN CAPITALS ...   *DR. STOERK*
Zuname/Vorname/Dienstgrad des Sanitätsoffiziers
(In lateinischer Druckschrift und in grossen Buchstaben)

P.T.O.
Bitte wenden

† DELETE THAT WHICH IS INAPPLICABLE
Nichtzutreffendes durchstreichen

PSS 2196 5 48 1000m

62

III
PARTICULARS OF DISCHARGE
Entlassungsvermerk

THE PERSON TO WHOM THE ABOVE PARTICULARS REFER
Die Person auf die sich obige Angaben beziehen

WAS DISCHARGED ON (Date) ...... 16. 11. 47 .... FROM THE* .... HEER ....
wurde am (Datum der Entlassung)   vom/von der*   entlassen

RIGHT THUMBPRINT
Abdruck des rechten Daumen

CERTIFIED BY

NAME, RANK AND
APPOINTMENT OF CSM BAKER R.
ALLIED DISCHARGING
OFFICER IN
BLOCK CAPITALS

OFFICIAL
EMBOSSED
SEAL

Amtlicher
Einprägestempel

Einwohnermeldeamt Neubeckum .

Abgemeldet am 13.1.1949

J. A.

No. 2

* INSERT "ARMY", "NAVY", "AIR FORCE", "VOLKSSTURM" OR PARA-MILITARY
ORGANIZATION, e.g. "R.A.D.", "N.S.F.K.", ETC.
Wehrmachtteil oder Gliederung der die Einheit angehört, z.B. "Heer", "Kriegsmarine",
"Luftwaffe", "Volkssturm", "Waffen SS", oder "R.A.D.", "N.S.F.K.", u.s.w.

Einwohnermeldeamt Neubeckum
Gemeldet am 18.12. 1948
als Urlauber.

J. A.

Lebensmittelkarten bis ein-
schließlich 13. 1. 1949 erteilt.
Neubeckum, den 18.12. 1948

40.- M. PAID ON DISCHARGE

SIGNED

PAYMASTER

Polizeistation 7
Neubeckum
Gemeldet am 18. Dezember 1948
als Urlauber
(Striewski)
Polizei-Meister.

Abgemeldet am 13. Januar 1949

63

Certificate No. **BNA** 31118　　　　Home Office No. B. 6___.

BRITISH NATIONALITY ACT, 1948.

CERTIFICATE OF NATURALISATION

Whereas　　　　　　Alfred Bojanitz

has applied to one of Her Majesty's Principal Secretaries of State for a certificate of naturalisation, alleging with respect to　him self the particulars set out below, and has satisfied the Secretary of State that the conditions laid down in the British Nationality Act, 1948, for the grant of a certificate of naturalisation are fulfilled :

　　　Now, therefore, the Secretary of State, in pursuance of the powers conferred upon him by the said Act, grants to the said

　　　　　　Alfred Bojanitz

this Certificate of Naturalisation, and declares that upon taking the Oath of Allegiance within the time and in the manner required by the regulations made in that behalf he　shall be a citizen of the United Kingdom and Colonies as from the date of this certificate.

　　　In witness whereof I have hereto subscribed my name this 20^{el} day of

April　,19 54 .

HOME OFFICE,　　　　　　　　　　　　　　 J. Anderson

LONDON.　　　　　　　　UNDER SECRETARY OF STATE

PARTICULARS RELATING TO APPLICANT.

Full Name	Alfred BOJANITZ.
Address	Hollacombe House, Hollacombe, Wembury, near Plymouth, Devon.
Profession or Occupation	Builder's Labourer.
Place and date of birth	Beubeckum, Germany.　1st August, 1913.
Nationality	German.
Single, married, etc.	Married.
Name of wife or husband	Anna.
Names and nationalities of parents	Elias and Maria BOJANITZ (Yugoslav).

(For Oath
see overleaf.)

Oath of Allegiance

I, *Alfred Bojanitz*

swear by Almighty God that I will be faithful and bear true allegiance to Her Majesty, Queen Elizabeth the Second, Her Heirs and Successors, according to law.

(Signature) *Alfred Bojanitz*

Sworn and subscribed this 27 day of *a/une* 1954 , before me,

(Signature) *J. Finnigan*

Justice of the Peace for *Devon*.
A Commissioner for Oaths.

Name and Address
(in Block Capitals)
JAMES. FINNIGAN
LILAC. COTTAGE, PLYMSTOCK. DEVON.

Unless otherwise indicated hereon, if the Oath of Allegiance is not taken within one calendar month of the date of this Certificate, the Certificate shall have no effect.

HOME OFFICE
26 AUG 1954
REGISTERED

65

Once the war had ended honest hard work paid its dividends for those who wished to remain in England.

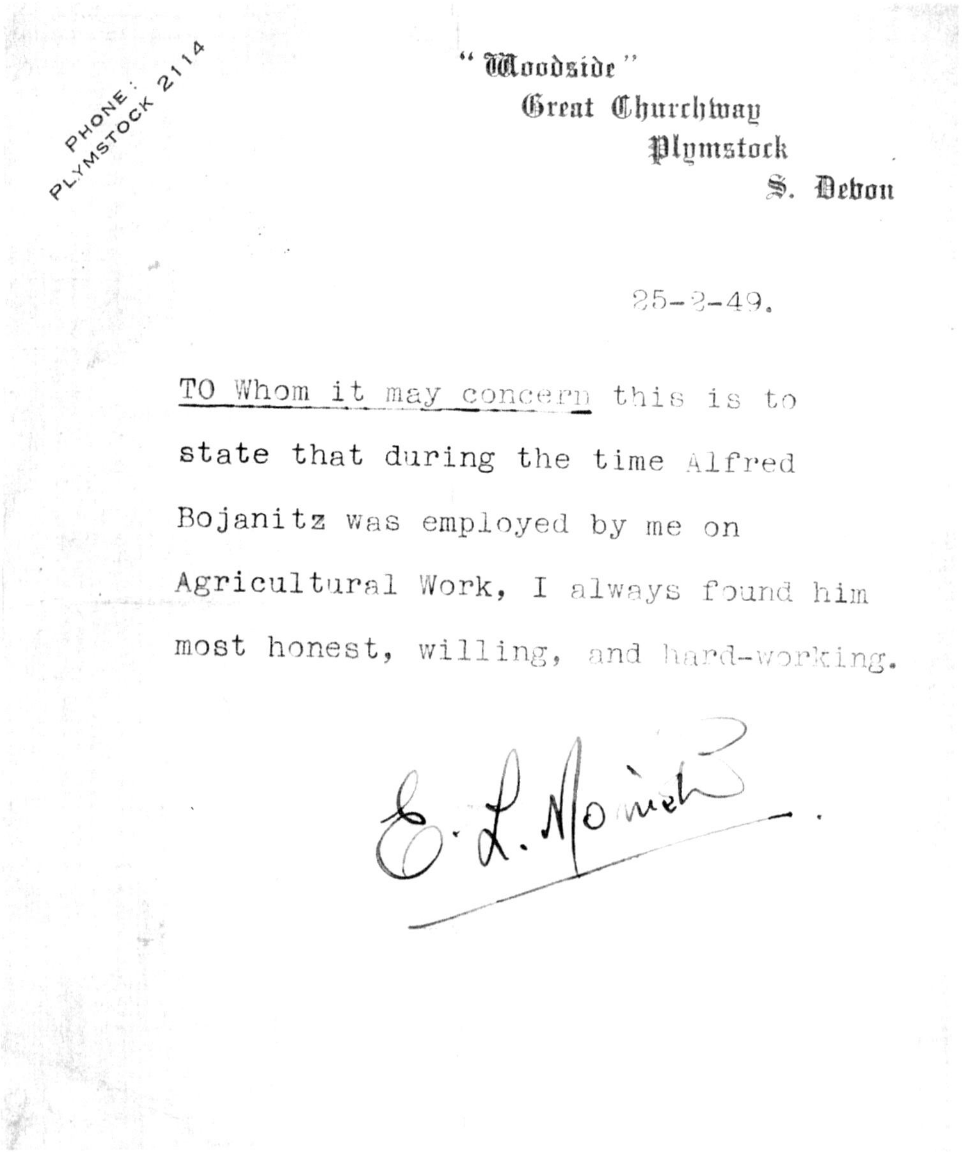

PHONE:
PLYMSTOCK 2114

"Woodside"
Great Churchway
Plymstock
S. Devon

25–2–49.

TO Whom it may concern this is to state that during the time Alfred Bojanitz was employed by me on Agricultural Work, I always found him most honest, willing, and hard-working.

E. L. Mowich

Whilst my father was in Germany Father Augustus Hegenkötter sent his greetings for the New Year and the peace of the Christ Child. Augustus asks if things are better in England or in his native country.

Patience was rewarded. My parents were married in St. Mary's Church, Brixton on August 28th 1948. The ceremony was conducted by Rev. Powell.

The bridesmaid, Elizabeth Gosling, later became Mrs. O'Neil who ran Plymstock Broadway florist shop.

Mrs. O'Neil (Elizabeth Gosling) recalls .....

Initially, Brixton Lodge (Kitley Camp) was used as a detention centre for Black Americans during the war. Mrs. Ivy Gosling (Elizabeth's mother) ran a canteen for troops. The canteen, near St. Mary's Church, Brixton, later became the Y.M.C.A. In recent times it has been used as a day nursery.

During its second stage during the war, Kitley Camp was used for housing Italian Prisoners of War. They brought their crafts and skills with them. Elizabeth recalls that some prisoners made wooden toys. With great delight she remembers a toy comprised of a model chicken perched on a table tennis bat. When Elizabeth pulled a string on the reverse of the bat the chicken pecked imaginary (or applied) corn. Kitley Camp was next used for German Prisoners of War who also brought their individual crafts and skills with them. In particular Elizabeth remembers that Alfred made beautiful patterned slippers from coloured cord. He sold them to locals for half a crown. Elizabeth remembers a lovely Christmas service the prisoners organized at the invitation of Reverend Powell.

Elizabeth's father, Mr. Cecil Gosling, worked in Wembury for Devon County Council. He came to know the villagers. He also knew Edna in her connection with Brixton Church as a choir member and relief organist during that difficult period.

On 28th August, 1948, at St. Mary's Church, Brixton, Cecil gave the bride away, Reverend Powell conducted the service and Mrs. Mutron was organist. Edna chose 'Jesu, joy of mans' desiring' by J.S. Bach for her wedding music. Elizabeth remembers her day as bridesmaid. Her dress in a shade of light sweet pea had been especially made for her. The headband of tiny paper flowers was a feature of post war economy. The reception was held in the Y.M.C.A and Mrs. Ivy Gosling provided the much appreciated catering.

Mrs. Ivy Gosling

Elizabeth Gosling

The recollections of Hermann Beeck

Hermann Beeck was a Prisoner of War at Chaddlewood prisoner of War Camp. He was born in Wanne-Eickel, Westfalia, in December 1923. Wanne-Eickel was completely destroyed in the war.

The church Hermann remembers .....
Maria Kirke (St. Mary's) in Wanne-Eickel.

Having been influenced by the Hitler Youth Movement and having absorbed some of the ideals, Hermann volunteered to join the German army when he left school. By volunteering he was given the privilege of deciding which unit he would join. He decided to join the signals unit and trained at Osterbruch. As he was a mere 'batman' at that time he was fortunate in not being amongst those who were sent to Russia. He was commissioned to join a machine gun battalion heading for the Channel Islands. Whilst on their way they raided the French coast and during that time Hermann was promoted to Sergeant (Fahrenjungen Officier). In this capacity he spent six weeks in Guernsey and then joined his battalion in Jersey. During this time of occupation Islanders and German soldiers alike made the best of things.

The residents were tolerant and bartering went on. Hermann was billeted in a cottage where a carpenter lived. Sometimes Hermann received bunches of grapes from him in exchange for cigarettes.

The battalion in Jersey. Hermann, in the third row from the front, is standing behind the third man from the left in the second row.

Left:
Early scenes in German
occupied Jersey.

Right:
Hermann as signal officer.

Left:
Sports
Day.

One evening Hermann and another soldier broke the rules and went to a night club. Later in the evening a senior officer paid a surprise visit to the club. Hermann was fortunate to escape through a back window but his companion wasn't so lucky and was placed under disciplinary procedures. He was sent North, perhaps to lose his life in the fighting.

Hermann's stay in Jersey was short. He was captured and taken to a special Prisoner of War Camp in Devizes. At this camp prisoners who had been members of 'The Hitler Youth Movement' were re-educated to face the true facts. Many Prisoners of War were traumatized when presented with facts backed by documentary films on war crimes.

At Devizes the prisoners of War built the camp. During their time at the camp they learned basic English.

Hermann Beeck as a young soldier ... captured early in the war he was saved much trauma or a worse fate...

From Devizes Hermann was taken to Hatherleigh in North Devon. The Prisoner of War Camp was situated near a sewage complex at Bridgerule. Whilst

A temporary graveyard in Jersey for German soldiers killed in Europe during the period Hermann's battalion was there.

Prisoners of War in front of one of the buildings they had constructed at the Devizes Prisoner of War Camp. Hermann Beeck is third from the right. The first man on the left also went on to Devon for he appears in the centre of the photograph of the Chaddlewood work party in the first section of this book.

there he worked on a local farm owned by George Crocker. Next he was moved to Saltram Park prisoner of War Camp at Chaddlewood. As a Prisoner of War he worked at Maristow, Roborough for a time.

After the war Hermann worked in the dairy department of the Co-op. At a birthday party of a work colleague he met his future wife Pat Dow. After they were married they worked as stewards for The British Legion in Brixton for three years. Hermann also became a member of TocH and played his part in wheeling patients from Mount Gould Hospital to Central Park for the Plymouth Argyle match. Hermann had various occupations. He has been a self employed roundsman baker covering many of the Dartmoor villages.

Stewards for the British Legion at Brixton.

Members of the men's section of the Plymstock branch of TocH

Recognized men in the above photograph:

Back row (first on the right) Jim Symons, (second on the right) William Johns, (third on the right) Hermann Beeck.

Front row (second from the right) John Purdy, (first on the left) Mr. Crow.

In the second photograph recognized members are in the same places.

The recollections of Mr. John Casley .....

A former resident of Hollacombe, John attended Wembury Primary School until 1940 when he went to Plympton Grammar School. He remembers how, at the end of the school playground, two men dug out a rather gloomy air raid shelter in a week. Escorted by Miss Axworthy, Miss Maynard, and occasionally Miss Jarvis, the children went to the shelter whenever the air raid siren sounded. Hurricane lamps provided light in the shelter. Miss Maynard used to get the children singing to raise their spirits. John recalls that eight year old Gilda Philips was the centre of attention amongst the pupils, the boys in particular, as she had the exciting background of having been evacuated from Alderney.

John remembers how every member of the school clambered onto the playground wall to watch the marine band go by. The men's faces showed relief at having finished the Ford Road climb. Behind the bandsmen followed a company of seventy marines, all of whom were billeted at Langdon Court.

Sadly marines from this company were killed on H.M.S Trinidad in a torpedo accident. "They were wonderful men who helped entertain the villagers by providing live band dances on Saturday nights" John commented.

Miss Maynard, who like Miss Axworthy taught two generations of children, taught the children the French National Anthem. In John's words "This was sung in a show of patriotic fervour for their fast disappearing allies."

News of war time events affected the children. John remembers how they knew it was a tremendous loss for Britain when H.M.S Hood was sunk. When the 'Bismarck' was located and destroyed there was a 'triumphant uproar' for they knew it to be victory for England. They had extra playtime to 'celebrate' the event. Whilst Wembury missed most of the bombing, apart from explosions of a landmine in the fields to the east of Church Road, when two empty houses were destroyed on the cliff tops to the east of St. Werburgh's church, Hollacombe was a frequent target.

The home of John and his parents, at the end of Hollacombe Brake, was situated above Cofflete Creek with Traine Woods leading down. Decoys had been set at Steer Point and at the sound of a siren they would light up. German bombs were dropped as the pilots mistook the River Yealm estuary for Plymouth Sound.

A 250 pound bomb landed in John's garden and blew out the glass of the greenhouse and house and smashed crockery that ended up on the kitchen floor. John and his mother had gone down to the shelter. His father was still in bed and when the bomb had exploded John and his mother had thought his father had met certain death. Meanwhile his father's thoughts were that the shelter had been hit and in his anguish he ran bare foot across the broken china which caused problems. The creature who escaped completely unscathed was their tethered goat. John mentioned how "Come the dawn, the goat was absolutely untouched and bleating away as usual. A quirk of blast effect repeated often elsewhere!"

Hollacombe also received two thousand pounder bombs, countless incendiaries and some phosphorous bombs. John salvaged three unignited incendiary bombs from the mud at Cofflete Creek. Their neighbour, the local A.R.P (Air Raid Precautions) man arranged for bomb disposal experts to remove them.

Footnote: My mother Edna's recollections reinforce John's account. A bomb fell some yards from her home and caused a piece of shrapnel to embed itself in her nose. She had to go to the Red Cross Station at Plymstock. When she returned with her nose bandaged she looked like Pinocchio.

When this happy scene was taken in 1937 no one imagined a 250 pound bomb would land there a few years later. In this photo we see John, his cousin, his mother, and his Aunty holding the shafts.

After playing at Cofflete Creek, this photo was taken in 1937. John (left back row) and his cousins, pictured here, could not venture there during the war years.

John recalls various aircraft crashes. A Hunbell ITL crashed near Roborough. Three aircraft fell in Wembury. In broad daylight in the summer of 1940 a Westland Lysander developed engine trouble and made a free landing east of Ridge Cross. Although it landed in Wembury Parish, it momentarily bounced into Brixton Parish. The pilot and the observer were unhurt.

John and his parents. 1936.

In 1942 a Spitfire crash landed above Knighton Hill to the south of the reservoir. Being small, John was allowed to crawl under the damaged wing with a rope to enable the middle aged aircraftsman attach a sling to the mobile crane. John was duly rewarded with a chunk of plexiglass and the much prized rear view mirror of the cockpit. Of 1943 John tells the tale of another Spitfire crash landing in the field parallel and to the east of Knighton Hill. The plane clipped the hedges of the road near the Alms Houses and landed in the field behind Four Corners. The pilot was unscathed. Then there was the time when there was momentary panic in Hollacombe when residents thought an enemy parachute had come down. This turned out to be a barrage balloon.

John's final recollection of Wembury during war time was of the fund raising for Mrs Churchill's aid to Russia, the R.A.F benevolent fund and a host of other causes his parents went around the village making house to house collections. Nothing was thrown away during that time. At Lady Walker's invitation a collection point for clothing, pots and pans and other practical items, was set up at Wembury House. Finally, in words that draw us into the atmosphere of those times John went on to say:

"... In those days the people of Wembury got together as never before, or since. The concerts in the Village Hall, local talent, Mrs Milden singing 'Whitewings', Mrs Ayres singing 'Marta', me singing 'My Blue Braces', the navy singing their version of 'The Belle of Wembury Beach', everyone pulling together by a common purpose. Dare I say I regret those days have gone?" says John in words that draw us into the atmosphere of those times.

Happy times did return. In this photo we see John and his wife, local girl, Muriel Harvey.

The former Primary School at Ford Road, Wembury

The Alms Houses near Thorn, Wembury

This 1940 photograph includes a missing link in Wembury's history. A close up of the wall reveals (opposite) .....

Royal Marine Bandsmen lost on HMS Trinidad March 1942: Harold Davis (Band Master), Stanley Bennett, Ronald Brewer, Albert Field, Cecil Mason, Leonard Bonfield, Wilfred Collinge, Arthur Glass, Charley Sullivan.

Cofflete Creek

Knighton Hill

Wembury House

Ridge Cross where a pill box once stood and where
a Westland Lysander made a landing.

Mary Towill (Mrs. Dyer) recalls .....

Mary recalls that Edna Sly and another girl worked at New Barton Farm and then at Old Barton Farm as land girls. Mary's father, William Towill was a member of the Home Guard. The company used to meet in the Parish Room at Ford Road.

Mr Towill was also a Coast Guard and it was his duty to be on guard in the building with a view of the sea near the Mill Cafe. It was also his duty to walk the cliffs to Wembury Point armed with a gun. He shared his coast guard duties with another coast guard, Mr Richardson, who lived in a bungalow in Church Road, just before the turning into Cliff Road from Church Road. Mary remembers going to the Mill Cafe with her father to collect their tray of bread and jam and a pot of tea, to take back to their duty hut.

Whenever an air raid was on, neighbours used to come to Mary's home at Brownhill Lane. This was because the bungalow had a flat roof, inconspicuous from the air. As a child at that time Mary experienced no sense of danger. She well remembers the day before she started school for the first time in January 1941. Plymouth was blitzed and the bits and pieces, from Pophams and other major stores, blew into Wembury. Three fields away from the end of Brownhill Lane was a 'fire field' where timber was to be burned as a decoy should ever the need arise. In that connection the remains of a building are to be found in the field.

Mr and Mrs Towill bought their home in the 1930's. Their closest neighbours were the Smallridges at West Wembury Farm and the Nelders at New Barton Farm. Miss Nelder married Mr Erscott at a later period when he was gardener for Major *Studholm at Wembury House.

Like John Casley, Mary remembers air raid training and gas mask practice at Wembury Primary School. There were two air raid shelters near the school. One they approached through a hole in the wall and down steps. The other, next to the Parish Room still exists at this present time.

Mary commented " ... Blackouts were a part of everyday life until I was eight years old (1943). In that same year I recall recall seeing prisoners lean against their huts under trees. The huts were there for years afterwards. Like my parents I had a ration book. Theirs had a cream cover and mine a blue."

Mary's memories tie in with the recollections of others of blackouts, ration books and Italian Prisoners of War at Kitley Camp. Mary searched her attic and found her ration book ...

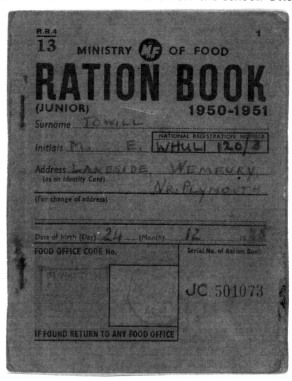

*Footnote: A quiet kind hearted man, Major Studholm M.P. later became Sir Henry Studholm.

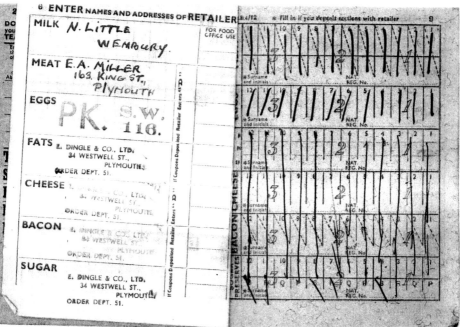

MILK N. LiTTLE WEMBURY.

MEAT E.A. MILLER 163. KiNG ST., PLYMOUTH

EGGS PK. S.W. 116.

FATS E. DINGLE & CO., LTD. 34 WESTWELL ST., PLYMOUTH ORDER DEPT. 51.

CHEESE E. DINGLE & CO., LTD. 34 WESTWELL ST. PLYMOUTH ORDER DEPT. 51.

BACON E. DINGLE & CO., LTD. 34 WESTWELL ST. PLYMOUTH ORDER DEPT. 51.

SUGAR E. DINGLE & CO., LTD. 34 WESTWELL ST., PLYMOUTH ORDER DEPT. 51.

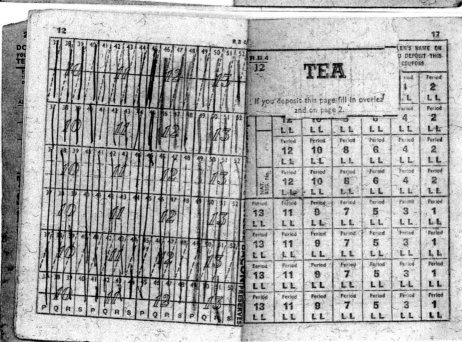

TEA

If you deposit this page fill in overleaf and on page 2.

Reminders .....

Reminders of the Second World War are to be found locally. On Wembury Beach the foundations of two pillboxes exist. Another is located in the garden of Bay Cottage at the bottom of Church Road. Several pillboxes have been dismantled. Mr. Kenneth O'Connor remembers that a pillbox existed in the middle of Wembury Road at Ridge Cross. For for some time after the war the bus driver had the unenviable task of manoeuvring the bus around this obstacle.

I remember a pillbox in the garden of Mr and Mrs Sellick's bungalow, the property on the left of the main road after leaving Train Road at the Hollacombe end. A similar pillbox is to be seen at Staddiscombe in the field parallel to Hooe Lane.

Pillboxes were placed at strategic points to enable soldiers or auxiliaries within to fire at the enemy from the embrasures. Mr. Godfrey Smallridge recalls that Mr. Towill and Mr. Richardson often acted as watchmen in the pillboxes.

Can you spot the pillbox in the garden of Bay Cottage?

In the following photograph the cross marks the foundation of the former pillbox. Above it is the building once occupied by the coastguards Mr. Towill and Mr. Richardson, and in recent decades used as a National Trust shop.

And the people ..... Edna Bojanitz keeping a watchful eye on her niece Mary Sly (centre), Heather McCubbin (left) and daughter Maria (me) right.

Another pillbox foundation at Wembury Beach (below the tree).

The pillbox at Hooe Lane, Staddiscombe.

Air raid shelter next to the Parish Room at Ford Road, Wembury

Air raid shelter, Cliff Road, Wembury

Heinz

Meanwhile at West Wembury Farm, Mr. Godfrey Smallridge recalls .....

A Prisoner of War named Heinz worked for them at West Wembury Farm. Heinz was at Merrafield Prisoner of War Camp at Plympton during the time he worked on the farm. Originally Merrafield was an army head-quarters. When the army was diverted off, the former headquarters, situated near Lyneham House, was used as a Prisoner of War Camp. Mr. Cadbury's aeroplane runway was also near the camp.

The Prisoners of War arrived at West Wembury Farm at approximately 9.30 a.m each day. Their lorry was driven by a private driver and there were no guards as the prisoners were trustworthy. They were only too glad to get out of the camp to work.

Whenever a farmer required workers he simply telephoned a camp and booked a number of men for the days they were required. Heinz was one of these seasonal workers.

The Germans worked hard. They knew land and country skills even to the degree of telling the time of day by using their hand and a raised finger as a makeshift sun dial. They were always ready to be collected at 4.00 p.m.

During another season another German worked at West Wembury Farm. His name was Adolf and he was at Lyneham Camp. He was a large chap, a butcher by trade. Like the rest of the German prisoners of War, he was far more reliable than the Italians.

Godfrey recalls village life during those years and he remembers Mr. Henshaw *the butler at Wembury House driving a Daimler car.

Miss Walker of Wembury House was a 'friend of Wembury School' (this being the school in Ford Road). The Sports Day was held at Wembury House with Miss Walker generously providing tea for all and prizes for winners of the races.

Miss Walker

Godfrey recalls that Escalonia* was owned by Mr and Mrs Algate. Mrs. Algate (nee Axworthy) was a teacher at the school from the 1920's until the early 1960's. She taught two generations of children.

During the war time period the blacksmiths were Jack, who did the shoeing, George, who owned one horse, one cow and a couple of bullocks, Nixy (Nicholas) who had a horse and cart. Their brother Dick was not in good health. They owned three fields at the top of Knighton Hill and some thirteen acres at Hollacombe.

*These recollections tie in with those of Johannes Löscher.

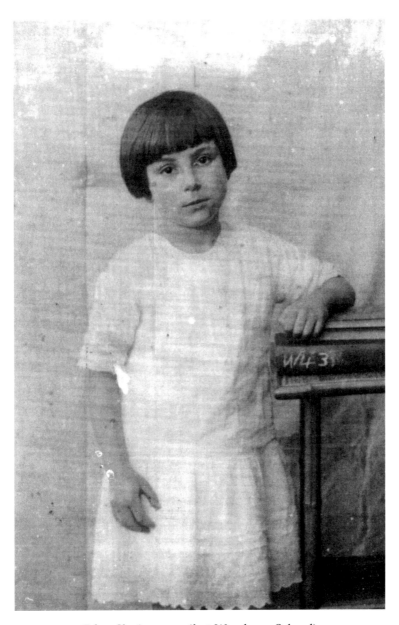

Edna Sly (as a pupil at Wembury School)

Farming Scenes .....

Harvest time at West Wembury Farm.
Godfrey Smallridge's mother is in the
foreground.

Rocket the cart horse. This photo
was taken in 1940 when Rocket
was twenty-one. He was the
children's favourite throughout
the nineteen-forties and fifties.

1937: hay making in a field owned by Mr. and Mrs. Shepherd at Train Farm.
The busy workers are John Casley, his parents, aunty, his cousin.

(above)
Summer 1998. Godfrey is 'arrested'
by his Grandson James.

(right)
James, his sister Charlotte and
Rebecca Bojanitz dance among the
flowers.

The recollections of Doris Congdon (Mrs. Russell) .....

Doris, of Plymstock, was seventeen when war broke out. She worked in Dingles and after it was bombed she joined the Land Army. Doris and her local friend Winnie McDonald went to Constantine, near Falmouth, to work at Popenwith farm. This was a long way from home. Doris and her parents lived at Plymstock road in a bungalow use as a Doctor's surgery.

After a period at Constantine Doris continued her Land Army work in Plymstock. She worked at Mr. Rowland's farm, 'Home Farm' in Rocky Park Road. Joyce Thomas worked alongside her and Doris was there for three years or more. Joyce lived in a cottage situated behind Home Farm. The girls had to take the cart horse to Elburton to be shod. Mr Truscott, the blacksmith, was a jolly little man. *His father's shop was a family business. The girls used to ride the horses along the route past Plymstock Church and up Dunstone Road. Doris remembers one day in particular when on the return journey her horse stopped to relieve itself near a rather elite crowd at the end of an R.A.F funeral procession. Never was a young lady so embarrassed in all her life!

At Home Farm there were part time helpers ... earlier in the war Italians and later German Prisoners of War, from Saltram. The girls did talk to the lads who were able to communicate in broken English. Doris remembers a young man called Paul being only seventeen. An Italian called Enrico was another prisoner who made a lasting impression. "The prisoners were very good seeing as they were in a strange country" commented Doris.

From Home farm Doris went on to work at Train Farm Wembury. They travelled by lorry each day and worked from 8.00 a.m until 5.00 p.m. William Russell (Doris' husband) was a Plymouth man who joined the R.A.F. for the duration of the war (1939-1945). He was in the Western Desert in Tripoli when, in 1943,he was sent to Roehampton Hospital for Tropical Diseases. Initially he had been a dispatch rider and was stationed in the desert for four years.

Doris and William were married after the war. Land army work continued for a time after the war until people came back and returned to 'normal' life.

William Russell (R.A.F).

*The Old Smithy is currently the florist shop.

A photograph of the Land Army arm band Doris wore.

At Train Farm.....

Doris, wearing her Land Army uniform.

Some pages from Doris's book ...

air. The Land Army member is bound to be mobile. She is willing to go where she is sent.

It is hoped, therefore, that it is quite clear that the Women's Land Army is not for those who are already employed in agriculture, but for the volunteers who are willing to make agriculture their war-time profession.

Some 12,000 women have already enrolled in this magnificent Army, led by the Honorary Director, the Lady Denman, D.B.E. It is hoped that as a result of this book thousands more will join, for work on the land is a form of national service of incalculable benefit to the country at the present time.

Listen to part of the message of the Rt. Hon. R. S. Hudson, P.C., M.P., the Minister of Agriculture and Fisheries, to the Women's Land Army in October 1940. He said:—

" The events of the past 6 months have made increased food production at home even more urgent. Total war is a war of endurance, and to ensure winning it we must make the most use of all our resources, especially the land. Milking the cows, feeding the pigs and the poultry or

driving a tractor, day after day, is unspectacular and at times may seem to you very dull.

" But without the food you help to produce the bravery of the fighting services would be of no avail and the machinery in our munition factories would be silent and still. Famine could achieve what no bomb or blitzkrieg or invading force will ever bring about. It is your vital task to see that such a thing could in no conceivable circumstance arise, and is driven even further from the realms of possibilities."

are accepted for enrolment in the Women's Land Army. Volunteers are placed, as first choice, in employment in their county of enrolment, if employment offers there. They are only asked to go farther afield if no local employment offers *or* if the need for their services is greater elsewhere.

Application Forms

Each applicant for enrolment is required to complete application form No. W.L.A. E. & W. 1. (See Form A.)

Interviewing

Applicants, who should be women of good physique between the ages of 18 and 40 (except in very special cases), are interviewed by members of the Land Army panel of interviewers for the county, and if considered suitable for service on the land, are accepted and formally enrolled.

BEFORE starting on this chapter proper may I put two personal suggestions to readers?

1. If *you* were in the Land Army at the beginning of the war, and have been trained, and were doing well in the job, but had to resign for private reasons, do apply again now, if you are free, for you are badly needed.

2. Many women enrolled at the beginning of the war. Some of their forms may have been lost through enemy action or some other war emergency. If you are one of those who have never had a reply to the original form you filled in, do apply immediately to the County Secretary, whose address you will find in Chapter IX.

Now for prospective members.

Enrolment full-time mobile volunteers accepted only.

Only volunteers who can offer full-time mobile service (that is, service in any part of the country)

18

VOLUNTEERS may be given training if the County Secretaries feel that they need it, and this may be done either (*a*) on a farm, or (*b*) at a Training Centre (*i.e.*, at an Agricultural College or Farm Institute). If, however, the volunteer has had some experience, she may be sent straight into vital employment. It may be also that the volunteer will be considered suitable to go into some type of agricultural employment which does not necessitate special training.

In the case of *farm* training, this may be on the farm on which the volunteer is afterwards going to work, or it may be on a training farm, and then the volunteer will subsequently be passed on to another farm.

Payments and Allowances

Volunteers who are accepted for training are sent for four weeks for a free course, either at an approved farm or at an Agricultural College or Farm Institute.

27

Board and lodging is paid for by the Government, and an allowance at the rate of 10s. per week, less National Health and Unemployment Insurance contributions, is made by the Government to the volunteer for her personal expenses.

Training on Farms

The farmers who take trainees for instruction must, of course, be those who have time to spare to give such instruction. Volunteers on such farms can be assured that they will receive genuine training.

The training may be carried out on farms where the volunteer can be given special instruction in milking, tractor-driving, or the care of stock and poultry, or on those market-gardens and private gardens where all-round instruction can be given under supervision. The trainee will not simply be used for the purpose of providing unskilled labour, nor will she be expected to stick to only one or two processes.

The trainee should take with her her insurance cards and her ration books, containing the proper number of coupons.

The course of training normally starts on a

Monday, and at least one clear week before the training is due the volunteer will receive a form (see D) signed by the County Secretary.

On the second day of each week of training a claim form will be sent by the trainee to the Finance Section of the Women's Land Army Branch at the Ministry of Agriculture and Fisheries. Claim forms should be filled in correctly, and, to help trainees, notes will be supplied by the County Secretaries at the beginning of the training.

The billeting fees will be paid by the Government in a similar manner, and claim forms will be provided for the persons doing the billeting. When, however, the Women's Land Army trainee is living in her own home, or that of her parents, no weekly billeting fee will be paid. A fee up to 10s. per week may, however, be paid in such cases to the farmer if he is providing meals for the trainee.

National Health, Pensions and Unemployment Insurance

Members of the Women's Land Army placed in training come within the scope of the National Health Contributory pensions and Unemployment Schemes. Any trainee who has not already got her

---

There are so many obvious things which get forgotten. The volunteer should always be punctual in her hours; she should not smoke about the place, especially in farm buildings; she should shut gates behind her; she should put tools back properly, so that the next person who wants them can find them; she should never leave a job half done just because she finds it difficult.

A farmer is not made in a month, and, after training, some girls are inclined to try to teach the farmer his business, often with unfortunate results. So if a volunteer has been taught a method different from the farmer's, she should always ask his permission before making the change. Farmers have no time to bother with fussy volunteers. They expect girls who have offered to do the work to carry it out without complaint.

Trying it Out

A volunteer who enrols to " see if she likes it " is a liability, not an asset. However patriotic she may feel, she does not help her country by enrolling in the Land Army unless she is certain she can stay the course.

It is quite a good plan to try carrying buckets full

of water for half an hour or more at a time, and then attempting to pitch earth onto a barrow and then onto a shelf about breast high for another hour or so, to see whether she can bear the aches and pains entailed. Farming work is not spectacular, but it does mean hard physical strain, but any girl who can endure it finds compensation in the knowledge that she is playing a very important part in National Service.

Dissatisfaction

Some farm jobs are monotonous, but they are essential to food production. The volunteer should do them thoroughly and systematically, for by putting her best into the work she will make it interesting.

If, however, she is not completely happy, or is dissatisfied in any way, she should not throw up her job hastily, or grumble to her fellow-workers. The matter should be taken to the farmer himself, the County Secretary consulted or the District Representative talked to, and in this way it is usually possible to get matters put right.

Make-up

Town girls on the whole use far more make-up

G

than country girls. The Women's Land Army volunteer should therefore be prepared to " tone down " her lips, complexions and nails considerably.

A certain amount of make-up may be used at parties and local village dances, but long nails are quite unsuited to work on a farm, especially when covered with bright crimson nail-varnish.

The volunteer will soon find that, as the other girls from the village do not use make-up, she will prefer not to use it herself, so as not to look conspicuous. She will find, too, that she will get such a healthy colour to her cheeks that rouging will not be necessary!

Lending a Hand

Be prepared to do some useful work in the village during your spare time. It may be that you can get into touch with the local representative of the W.V.S. and do some knitting. Perhaps you will be able to help by forming one of the personnel of the village First-Aid Point. You can be very useful, too, by putting your name down as one of the fire-watchers.

Some Land Army volunteers have taken on

definite voluntary jobs in the villages. At least one is organising the local branch of the County Library, and is very much liked and appreciated as a result.

Socials

Join the local Women's Institute, and go to their meetings if they are held at a convenient time. Go to any socials there may be in the village, and try to fit in naturally. Don't push yourself, and so spoil things. Take part in all such activities in a humble manner, and help to break down any prejudice there may be against women on the land. Each volunteer can do her part to ensure smooth working and to help in securing the good name of the Women's Land Army.

Maids

When living at a farm where a maid is kept, the volunteer should remember that she also is employed by the farmer, and not by herself. She should not therefore expect the maid to wait on her, nor should she give the maid extra work and extra bother.

Sticking To It

The Land Army is judged by its members. A good volunteer is a good advertisement.

Every volunteer should remember that money has been spent on her equipment and training, to make her a *a specialist* for a vital job. She should not, therefore, *ever drop out.* She must feel that *she* is feeding the nation. If she drops out, someone may starve.

Further, wherever a recruit or a full Women's Land Army volunteer gives up, she represents a dead loss to her county, and her county cannot afford dead losses in a war like this.

There is the example to think of, too. If one volunteer gives up, it has an effect on others. Recruits coming along get to know, and so " rot " may set in.

The Land Army must have a motto—" Stick to It."

Girls who had to resign in the early days of the war for a good reason, or just to change their jobs, or even to go home, are wanted—they should, therefore, if reliable, offer their services once more, for they are certainly needed.

Training given at the Government's expense will thus *not* be wasted, nor will the experience gained be lost.

CHAPTER XI

USEFUL HINTS AND TIPS

Remedy for Roughened Hands

Put 1 ounce of olive oil and 1 ounce chopped beeswax into a jar in the oven until melted. Cool and, when easy to handle, roll into a ball. Rub lightly into the hands after washing. A little oat flour will remove greasiness.

Making Shoes Waterproof

Cut up a little beeswax and put into a jar. Cover with a little castor oil or neat's-foot oil. Stand in a warm place till wax is melted. Stir thoroughly. Allow to cool. If too thick add a little more oil.

To use, warm a little, apply with stiff brush while quite soft. Let that coat harden, warm boots slightly, and apply another coat. Neat's-foot oil alone is quite good.

To Make Gum Boots Slip on and Off Easily

Sprinkle French chalk inside the gum boots from time to time.

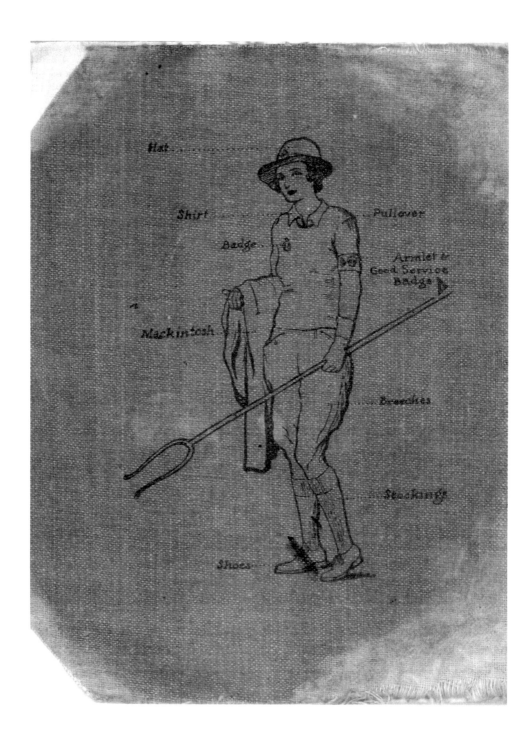

Hat

Shirt

Badge

Mackintosh

Pullover

Armlet &
Good Service
Badge

Breeches

Stockings

Shoes

The recollections of Roy and Ada Roberts (nee Steer) .....

Edna's cousin Ada was born in 1931. As a child she lived at Wembury Road, Elburton. When she was eight, or nine, a bomb landed nearby and she dived under her mother's morrison table (a shelter with a practical use). This saved her life as the force of the explosion scattered glass and debris everywhere. Ada also remembers morrison shelters being around at that time for home use. Several men were needed to piece together and erect these heavy shelters.

Ada attended Goosewell Primary School. She remembers walking, with her classmates, to the Blacksmith's Forge in Elburton for gas mask practice. After the practice the children were sometimes able to sneak into a nearby shop to buy 1d and 2d sweets before returning to school.

When she went on to Plymstock Secondary School the war was still happening. A year later, when the family moved to Plympton, she attended Plympton Secondary School at St. Maurice.

At Plympton she was out with a friend in Lucas Lane when an air raid took place. She was very frightened and ran home as fast as she could. Screaming to be let in, she hammered on the door. This was to no avail as her mother was out working and her step father was at the pub. The memory of the panic left its own scar. In particular, Ada remembers a nightmare occurring when she was fourteen or fifteen. She awoke screaming because in her dream the ceiling was about to cave in. Ada's father, William Steer (my Grandmother's brother) died in a tragic accident when Ada was five. Had he lived to see the war he would have continued in the Dockyard in the reserved occupation, as he was a boiler maker.

Ada's mother, Florence Mary Steer (nee Webber), had a cousin at Oke-hampton. Ada remembers going to Okehampton, with her brothers and sisters, to stay at his home when her mother re-married in 1944. The children gave him the nickname Uncle father for a time.

Ada was one of nine children, six of whom were in the forces during the war. William, Frederick and Frank were in the Navy. As he was in the medical corps Frank dealt with medical supplies. *Sydney, David and Audrey were in the Army in military service. Phyllis and Bertha were housewives. Bertha, who had married Fred Avent, a gardener at Wembury House where she worked, first settled at Stone Barton in Plympton.

Ada was able to leave school at thirteen because she was to be fourteen on September 5th and the school term started on September 6th. She worked in a confectioners at Plymouth Market. Her wage was fourteen shillings a week and the bus fare for the week was four shillings. She remembers that people bought sweets with their coupons. "It was all go on the days they received their new points" she said. Ada was eighteen when she married Roy at Plympton St. Mary Church in 1949. They lived at Grenville Road for a time.

*At Ada's funeral service in 2011 I met Professor Philip Steer. He informed me that his father Sydney was in the Navy (Fleet Air Arm).

John Henry Steer, his wife
Florence and their children

WESTERN EVENING HERALD

EXTRA FINAL EDITION

DAY,   EVENING HERALD,   FEBRUARY 15, 1937.

NEL FOR 4 HOURS.

BOILERMAKER'S NECK BROKEN.

ACCIDENT ON WAY FROM ELBURTON TO DOCKYARD.

A Devonport Dockyard boilermaker died from a broken neck at the Prince of Wales's Hospital, Greenbank-road, to-day, following an accident while cycling to work early this morning.

The dead man is Mr. John H. Steer, 3, Newton-terrace, Elburton, and he leaves a widow and several children.

The accident happened near Billacombe railway station about 6.30 a.m. a collision occurring between Mr. Steer's cycle and George Turner, 59, labourer, of no fixed abode, who was walking to Plymouth.

Plymouth St. John Ambulance was called, and Con. A. P. Harding of Plympton, was quickly on the scene, accompanying the injured man to the hospital.

FROM PLYMOUTH

DEVONPORT DENTIST FINED.

DRIVING WITHOUT DUE CARE AND ATTENTION.

PLYMOUTH COLLISION.

At Plymouth, to-day Henry Frederick Vere, dental surgeon, of St. James's-place, Devonport, was fined 10s. for driving a motor-car without due care and attention and ordered to pay 25s. costs.

Mr. Felix Goodman, who appeared for Vere pleaded Not guilty.

David Roseman, 27, Carlisle-terrace, Plymouth, said he was driving his motor car just after 2.45 a.m. along Citadel-road.

At the junction of Elliot and Athenaeum-streets a collision occurred with another motor-car when he was travelling at only ten miles per hour.

NEARLY OVERTURNED.

The other car, he said, came from Elliot street, which was a minor road

Wembury House gardener Frederick Avent outside his home at Knighton Hill.

Family connection.

Maria with Fred and Bertha's oldest daughter, Joan (Oxland).

Ada aged fifteen

Roy and Ada in 2000

Ada's husband Roy lived in Plympton from the age of ten. In 1938, at the age of fourteen, he left school to become a butcher's boy. He cycled on his carrier bike to deliver meat to customers in Plympton and the surrounding area. He did all this for a starting wage of ten shillings and sixpence. Roy made many trips to Chaddlewood House and Saltram House, both of which were to become Prisoner of War Camps; for Italian Prisoners of War in 1944 and German Prisoners of War later in 1945. Roy mentioned that Chaddlewood House has quite a history, having been built in the early 1800's. Roy learned that Indian Cavalry were billeted there during the First World War as well as the Second World War. He has clear memories of them exercising their horses; both horse and its rider were immaculately turned out. Fifty or more passed through Ridgeway, Plympton on several occasions in 1940 and 1941. "Regrettably I had no camera to record the spectacle" Roy commented.

A year later in November 1942 Roy's own turn came to join 'His Majesty's Forces'. As he had been a cadet in the A.T.C (Air Training Corps) Roy went into the RAF, reporting to R.A.F. Padgate in Lancashire (now Cheshire). On June 6th 1944 'Operation Overlord' took place and in August 1944 a hundred and thirty five Wing 2nd T.A.F (Tactical Air Force) of which Roy was a part, disembarked from Landing Craft (L.S.T's) at Arromanches in Normandy and proceeded in convoy to Carpiquet

Roy (first right) and his colleagues at RAF Broadwell, Oxon, 1946.

Roy was awarded various campaign medals ...

Campaign Medals (left to right):

(1) 1939-1945 Star.

(2) France Germany Star.

(3) War Medal.

(5) 'Libertie diex Aei'.

The 'Libertie diex Aei' was presented to many service men and women at various venues in Normandy in 1994. Roy and others were presented with their medals by the Lady Mayoress of Caen, at the Abbaye Aux Dames in Caen, in appreciation for operation 'Overlord'.

(4) Non Campaign medal in Roy's case: For joining the Royal Observer Corps 1958 and serving for thirty two years and retiring at the age of sixty-five. The role of the R.O.C was the monitoring and reporting of nuclear fall out. "Thankfully this never came to pass. Thank God!" Roy commented. R.O.C was stood down in 1991.

Airfield near Caen. Roy explained that from July 4th to July 7th, possession of this important airfield (that finally had fallen into allied hands) was violently disputed between the 3rd Canadian Division and the 12th SS Panzer Division, and eventually taken over by 2nd TAF in August 1944.

The recollections of Eileen and Maurice Hammett .....

Eileen whose maiden name was McCrum first met Maurice when he was stationed in Ireland for some ten months following his army training at Dorchester. Fortunately his time in Ireland took him to her home town of Banbridge, County Down, Northern Ireland. They married in Banbridge on July 3rd 1943 and as a married couple had only seven days together whilst Maurice was given leave before he was stationed in Burma. During that short spell Eileen travelled to Plymouth with Maurice so that she could meet his parents before he left. Meanwhile Maurice's brother George, who was in the navy was awarded the Distinguished Service Medal for his work on 'Motor Torpedo Boats'.

Maurice (cousin of Edna Sly) volunteered for the army when the Second World War broke out. He was in the Eleventh Devon Regiment. After completing their basic training in Dorchester the men were sent to the First Wiltshire Regiment or the First Devonshire Regiment. Whilst serving in the First Wiltshire regiment Maurice was given leave to marry Eileen. This was no easy matter as there had been

several instances of bigamy in Belfast and in Bainbridge itself. Maurice had to obtain proof of his single status from his parents in addition to needing their consent as he was only nineteen. Although leave was short he was able to ensure that Eileen had settled with his *parents George and Emma at Crabtree House, Plympton before he left for Burma.

Whilst local life continued as normally as possible Maurice's duties in the Burma Infantry took him to various places in India. He was in the Aracan where he helped the R.A.F drop supplies. Travelling in Dakota aeroplanes his task took him to the front line of Burma on three occasions.

Maurice well remembers his first task on land. He had to locate a map reference 'Hill 105'.

* I well remember visiting my Great Aunt Em and 'Uncle George' at Crabtree House. They both (George in particular) had a mischievous sense of humour. Emma was George Henry Sly's sister.

Eileen and Maurice on their wedding day, 3rd July 1943.

Emma Hammett (nee Sly)

George Hammett

OF
LE
OI
ea
by
by
all
Ag
-?
lua;(
ue
mfl
ver.
coa
gust)
si
as new
UAR
nomina
rs; super,

EVENING HERAI

& WESTERN EVENING NEWS

PLYMOUTH, FRIDAY, OCTO

NCED TO SIX MON

'IN A 40
lloon; hea
1 owner: &
ber; AUST
Saloon, i
te;y as new;
IN A 70 "H.
nominal mi
ition throug

lALL " VELO
adio heater.
it; choice of
.70
ARD 8 Tour
id attractive;
ighout; £290
0; genuine M
1 owne
ghout £299
AUSTIN 8
lent condition
FORD 8 ANG
acement eng

RD 9 Salo
onditioned:
ain; £230
D 8 de Lu
reconditione
out £220
ANDARI)
; imm

4-D(
s a
b (

ROVE RECORD-BREAKING BOAT TRAIN

Driver G. Hammett, of Crabtree House, Laira, and Fireman R. Luscombe of 42, Aylesbury-crescent, Whitleigh, on their return to North-road Station Plymouth, today, receive congratulations from Laira Shed foreman, Mr V. C. Joyner, on yesterday's record-breaking Plymouth-Paddington boat train run. Today is Mr. Hammett's 62nd birthday.

George Hammett hit the headlines on 8th October 1954.

From the window of the London-bound trains passengers often delighted in George's working model railway in his large garden at Crabtree House.

When he reached the summit he saw three lads lying there and thought to himself "Silly fools ... sunbathing". Then much to his horror he realized they were dead. A closer inspection revealed they had been shot. It was a gruesome task for Maurice to have to help bury the lads who, like him, were still in their teens.

The recollections of Miss Barbara Snell of Hollacombe .....

One of Barbara's first memories of war time years is of sitting alongside her friends on the anti tank landing protection on the beach. This was a kind of scaffolding. Seated on the bars the children loved to be splashed by the incoming waves. After the war Barbara's father bought the scaffolding after it had been dismantled.

Following night air raids the children of the area searched the fields for fragments of bomb shells (shrapnel) and took their find to school to barter and exchange among the other children.

During air raids Barbara slept in a cot with boards over the top in case the ceiling fell in. She attended Kirkley Primary School at Plymstock, run by Miss Viners. The children had to carry their individual gas mask to school and practice wearing it. The experience contributed to Barbara's claustrophobic feelings in confined spaces. If a siren sounded during school time the children were taken to a reinforced room that served as a bomb shelter.

At home Barbara's parents had a 'dug out' that was no more than a pit covered with timber and earth for protection and camouflage. Barbara had a makeshift bed in it. Like Mary Towill, Barbara remembers how at home, shutters were placed over the windows before anyone could switch on a light. This was to prevent aircraft pilots finding residential areas. 'Blackout' was an everyday word in their vocabulary. It was a good thing they kept to the rules as one night an enemy aircraft unloaded its bombs in a line in the fields below Hollacombe, just missing the row of houses.

Because Barbara was such a young child, her mother was able to buy bananas occasionally, much to the envy of neighbours. Barbara recalls that books of coupons, ration books, were used for petrol, food and clothing. They had to save coupons so that they could buy anything new to wear. People used their initiative to overcome difficulties and even made clothing from wartime balloon fabric and other war time

In this photograph Barbara, on the far left, sits next to Pamela Mitchell, two other friends and Bobby Mitchell at Thorn, Wembury. 'What happened to the waves?'' they well may ask.

material.

Richard and his daughter Dorothy (Clark).

Barbara remembers Land Army girls coming to cut cabbages in their field. This was because her father Russell was a smallholder producing food for the war effort. This status exempted him from 'call up' and he joined the Home Guard.

The recollections of Richard Folley .....

Richard was born in Ivybridge in 1903 and lived at number ten in Highland Street for many years. During most of his adult life he lived at Brixton.

Richard well remembers my father Alfred. He identified with him as they were of similar short stature.

Reverend Powell, the vicar of St. Mary's Church Brixton, was very good to the Prisoners of War. He used to take services at the Prisoner of War camp. In 1944 the prisoners were invited to services at St. Mary's church.

Richard recalls how, from the choir stalls, during the prayers, all he could see of Alfred was two hands on top of the pew. He found this amusing because he was a short person himself and in a similar predicament. If others happened to notice the amused glances that passed between 'the brothers', no one ever made comment.

The Prisoners of War helped with the Harvest Thanksgiving. On another occasion Reverend Powell invited the Prisoners of War to sing the National Anthem. As far as Richard recalls they sang English National Anthem but he is certain it was sung in German. At a Christmas church service Reverend Powell *asked the Prisoners of War to sing 'Stille Nacht'. Undoubtedly Reverend Powell would have mentioned the sacred moment on Christmas day, 1914, during the First World War, when German and English troops came out of their trenches in no man's land to play a football match, using a makeshift ball, on the frozen ground.

Then, united in spirit they either sang or listened to the first verse of Franz Grüber's setting of Joseph Mohr's poem, 'Stille Nacht, Heilige Nacht' (Silent night, holy night). Gifts of provisions were exchanged and toasts were drunk.

In the 1940's the local postman, George Mutron was organist. His wife was a member of the church choir. Apart from Richard himself who sang tenor, other choir members included Mrs. Ivy Gosling, her daughter Elizabeth, Owen Sharp, a gas fitter, who also sang tenor and his step daughter Nell Martin. The bass singers were George Paddon, Bert King from Yealmpton and Ern Kits from Elburton. "Ern Kits sang so loudly his voice must have carried to Elburton" Richard added with a chuckle. At that time there was a Yealmpton Choral Society renowned for their frequent rendering of Handel's Hallelujah chorus from 'The Messiah'.

As time went on local people became fond of the Prisoners of War, having come to realize they were ordinary lads caught up in events.

*My parents have mentioned the very moving performance of 'Stille Nacht' during the Christmas service. It ever remained my father's favourite carol.

The Home Guard

Richard has clear memories of his days in the Home Guard. Once a week he went to Plymouth for his training. This was because he was unable to attend the Home Guard Infantry training days at Elburton as it occurred on Sunday afternoons when he was at work. A gardener by trade he was responsible for growing produce in large commercial greenhouses at Elburton. Incorporated in the training in the Home Guard was learning how to use anti aircraft guns. The men practised with dummy guns in Plymouth Guildhall. Richard remembers one practice taking place on the balcony of an empty hotel at Plympton. There were numerous divisions of the Home Guard.

When Richard and his companions completed training, they had to go on duty at Staddon heights once a week. The site was near Jennycliff beyond the fort on the hill.

A military discipline .....

The sergeant, whose voice was thunderous, made it clear they were there under military terms. He kept them 'on their toes'. They had to obey orders immediately no matter how irrational those orders seemed. One example was of receiving instructions to arrive with their boots highly polished only to receive further instructions to dull them with dubbin after inspection. This happened on several occasions and one man, a cobbler by trade, swore that dubbin rotted the stitching.

There were fifty-four guns at Staddon Heights and Richard was on gun number two. He had to receive instructions from gunner number one as he was the man who had ear phones and radio contact. The missiles used in the guns were similar to torpedos. A regular manoeuvre was to fire out to sea. In the event of an air raid their objective would have been that of keeping enemy air craft away and preventing bombing of Plymouth. It was tough work manning the guns after a full working day.

Supper was at nine o'clock and drill finished at ten o'clock. If they were lucky their volunteer officer Grant Arnold would play the piano to relieve the stress. He was a clerk for the Corporation and also organist at St. Emmanuel Church in Plymouth.

Richard well remembers how it took several days to recover from one night of duty. The Home Guard uniform was khaki and included a great coat. The mackintosh was grey, boots and gaiters were black. The jackets had brass buttons that required vigorous polishing before coming on duty. A specially designed circle of leather could be secured behind the button to protect the fabric during polishing.

In the event of a man missing a night of duty he had to report for duty the following night. Two brothers in the Elburton division missed two nights in succession. Consequently military personages knocked on their door and ordered them into a truck. They were driven to Crownhill where they were ordered out of the truck. One brother had the audacity to speak his mind as this was happening. Their punishment was a long walk home. From that time they never again missed a night of duty.

The men at Staddon Heights .....

Sometimes Richard returned home from Staddon Heights sore with laughter. One chap always took a secret bottle of stout with him and hid it under his bed. The occasional swig relieved the monotony of the night. The men found it difficult to sleep as they had to keep their uniforms on in case there was an air raid. One man, who worked in a brewery was so fat he had to rely on his wife to put his boots on his feet and tie the laces. For that reason he 'slept' with his boots on at Staddon Heights.

Another member of The Home Guard was Mr. Dunn who had a habit of putting his spectacles on the shelf before 'retiring'. He always had difficulty finding them during blackouts. Percy Briscombe was another member and Myo Fellows was their Captain (a bit of a stickler).

Plymouth had a particularly bad air raid one night that lasted from 8.00 p.m until 2.00 a.m. A.T.S girls arrived with a bucket of hot tea. They ladled the tea into mugs for the men. During a bad air raid one home guard lost his nerve and kept shouting 'Don't leave me'. He was in such a state of shock during the bombing he had to be taken to the medical room. The poor man never returned for duty.

Richard was nicknamed 'The Little Commando' because his greatcoat came down to his ankles. One night, thus attired he went for a walk with a Home Guard colleague, Stuart Gold. Inadvertently they went out of bounds which set the alarm off. 'The Little Commando' was so startled he jumped into the hedge to hide from 'invaders'.

Stuart Gold obviously survived the event as his one hundredth birthday celebration was recorded in the Evening Herald in May 1998. During the 1940's Stuart Gold owned a builder merchants hardware shop in Whipple Street. Stuart's wife was hospitable and an interesting conversationalist, Richard commented.

Richard Folley was a boy of eleven when the First World War broke out. Three older brothers were killed in action. One brother, Archie, was presented with a silver medal by the King of Serbia. This honour was awarded because he bravely fought his way through a pack of wolves in dangerous regions in order to get supplies of food through to troops.

Post Script .....
Richard died peacefully in April 2000 at the age of ninety-seven.

Within the Community .....

In the following photograph are villagers in 1954. Perhaps someone can recall the event? Mr. Sellick, the Elim Church minister, is standing at the back of the marquee.

Recognized adults: Alfred Bojanitz (next to the post), Edna Bojanitz (first right in the same row). Next to her is her friend Lydia McCubbin. In front of Lydia the lady wearing the hat could well be Mrs. Channing of Hollacombe. Dolly Carn is seated two rows in front of Alfred Bojanitz. Mrs. Margaret Bannaford is left behind

Left: George Henry Sly and granddaughter Maria (me), 1952.

Below: Alfred, Edna, Maria and Michael, 1953.

Peter Lugar (child). Lydia's sister Pearl Walters (possibly with Simeon on her knee) is seated two rows behind Jeanette Milden (child).

Recognized children: Front row (left to right) ..... Jimmy Milden, Angela Lugar, Maureen Milden, Sylvia Furzland, Colin Carn, Alan May, Maria Bojanitz.

Second row (left to right): Jeanette Milden, Ivy Gibson, Nina Denson, Christine Brown, Ivor Carn, (probably) Leonard Jewell, Peter Lugar.

TOC H

My parents were members of Plymstock TocH. The meetings were held at 'The Cave'. This was a room that was entered through a green door in a rustic granite wall that existed half way down the hill of Church road, Plymstock, some yards from the church. The men held their meetings on Tuesday evenings and the ladies on Wednesday evening. Along with other TocH men my father used to wheel patients from Mount Gould Hospital to see the Argyle match.

TocH originated in the First World War in 1915. It was founded by Tubby Clayton and developed further by Peter Monie who came to work for TocH in 1922. The name TocH is an abbreviation of Talbot House, a name given to a large house in Poperinge in Belgium. It was established as a place of peace for soldiers, a refuge in the midst of war. Since then, in war and peace time, TocH has continued its Christian mission. It is a non-denominational organization that aims to break down the barriers of prejudice about others. Members recognize the symbol of the lighted lamp as the light of Christ. The four compass points incorporated in the prayer centred start to TocH meetings are:

1. Friendship. 'To love widely' and incorporate all in friendship.

TocH group and Plymstock Choral Society Dickensian Evening, Drake Circus:1968. Recognized people: Top left Edna Bojanitz, centre in feathered hat May Scoble, in front of her Freda Woods, to the right of the front row ... holding the wicker tray Rose Norman, holding the ribboned basket Pat Palmer.

Left: TocH caravan, Plymstock
Broadway ... providing tea
and coffee. Circa 1956.

Left: May Scoble at that time.

Right: May Scoble in recent times.
May passed away in 2002. She was in her
nineties.

Snapshots by May Scoble ...

Left to right: Freda Wood, Ethel Larkworthy, Evelyn Osborne (nee Manley), Rose Norman, Gwen Cross and in the front her friend Myrtle.

Back row, left to right: Ethel Larkworthy, Gwen Cross, Rose Norman.
Front row, left to right: Pat Palmer, Nurse Barbara Ashton, Emily Coakley.

2. Service. 'To build bravely'. To give personal service.
3. Fairmindedness. 'To think fairly'. To listen to the views of others and to find personal conviction.
4. The Kingdom of God. 'To Witness Humbly'. To acknowledge the spiritual nature of humankind, to practice the Christian way of life, and to help the truth prevail.

The recollections of Evelyn Manley (Mrs. Osborne).

Evelyn lived with her mother in Whitchurch near Tavistock. She taught at Plymouth Road Junior School in Tavistock. Today it is used as a health centre. During the war it was closed for a time to house evacuees from Plymouth and London. Children stayed at the school a short period until foster homes could be found. When this community project had ended and school started, the evacuees integrated with the other children, seated three to a desk.

Evelyn was on Plymouth Hoe with her mother when she met Samuel Osborne. In common with Evelyn and her mother Sam had a Cornish background. He used to visit them at week ends to get away from the bombing. He was a railway

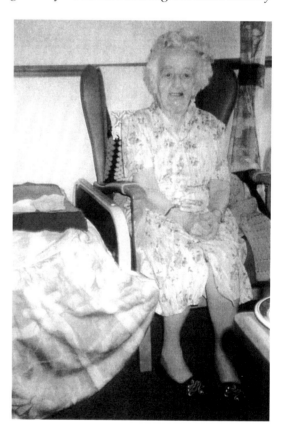

Evelyn at Springfields care home, Elburton. April 2003.

clerk and had been sent to Plymouth from Penzance during the war years. Evelyn

Members of Plymstock TocH and Mothers Union and associates. Magnet Cafe January 24th 1963.

Front row left to right: TocH members ... Eileen Purdy, May Scoble, Irene Lloyd, Gwen Cross, Beatrice Symons, Mary Strickland, Hilda Rowe, Ethel Larkworthy, Blanch Crocker, Mary Tremlett.

Back row left to right: TocH members Fern Scoble, John Purdy, Edith M Crow, Irene Williamson, Edna Bojanitz, and in the middle Reverend Noel Round, three congregation members followed by more TocH members Jim Symons, Nurse Ashton, Mrs. Hollman (M.U), Freda Wood, Alice Jewings (M.U), Winnie Symons, Hilda Lovell (M.U), Ivy Butler (M.U), Reverend Kenneth Newing.

Plymstock TocH ladies as Gypsies ready to entertain the senior citizens at St. Barnabas Church Hall, Stoke, on June 27th 1957. As part of the programme Evelyn Osborne wrote 'The lost bracelet', one of her many sketches.

Back row left to right: Gladys Wells, Winnie Simons, Frances Pow, Hilda Rowe, Freda Wood, Mary Knapton, Hilda Rowe's sister Mary (Strickland?), Ethel Larkworthy, Evelyn Osborne.

Front Row left to right: Gwen Cross, Michael Bojanitz, Edna Bojanitz, Eileen Purdy, Gladys Shannon.

Other TocH members during the 1950's and 1960's were: May Scoble, Nellie Johns, Nurse Barbara Ashton, Bertha Avent (Steer), Renie Lloyd, Betty Pick, Madge Rundle.

and Sam were married in St. Mary's Church Plympton in 1942. Eventually they settled in Rocky Park Road, Plymstock. Evelyn continued her teaching on a private basis. She taught Maria and Michael elocution in the 1960's.

TocH

The Women's section of Plymstock TocH gave a concert at Wembury Village Hall on Saturday, October 5th 1955 commencing at 7.30 p.m. Proceeds were in aid of the village hall building fund. Admission was seven shillings and sixpence. Programmes were duplicated by F.W. Salter, 37 Manor Road, Pomphlett.

Programme

1. a.The Happy Wanderer
The Choir   *Frederick W. Moller*
b. If I can help somebody
The Choir   *Alma Androzzi*

2. Dinner with the Squire (monologue
Evelyn Osborne   *Jan Stewer*

3. One Fine Day (solo)
Edna Bojanitz   *"Madam Butterfly"*

4. a. Moment Musical   *Schubert*
(Pianoforte duet)
May Scoble & Betty Pick
b. Gavotte   *Gussac*

5. A Peep into the Past (mime)
Edna Bojanitz   *Arranged by*
Evelyn Osborne & choir   *Evelyn Osborne*
Betty Pick

6. O For the Wings of a Dove (solo)
Michael Scoble   *Mendelssohn*

7. My Hero (solo)
Edna Bojanitz   *The Chocolate Soldier*

8. I Wonder
The Choir

9. "Brandy Balls" (one act play)
May Scoble, Nellie Johns, Alice Sophia Jackson, Betty Pick, Freda Woods,

TocH member Nellie Johns with Edna Bojanitz. Nellie, whose husband William (Billy) was sexton at St. Mary's Church Plymstock, was the Plymstock and district post lady for many years. By foot she covered Wembury as well as Plymstock. She used to take a roll of paper with her and scribble down wonderful poetry about the things she saw. I recall some of her poems about Langdon Woods and Laundry cottage. I believe some of her unpublished poems are in library archives and many were lent to a visitor and the identity of the visitor forgotten. Perhaps Nellie's poetic recollections of rural scenes will one day come to light. Nellie lived at Ingleside Residential Home in latter years and protested against the closing of the home. The story of the senior citizens journey to Downing Street is to be found in T.V and Newspaper archives.

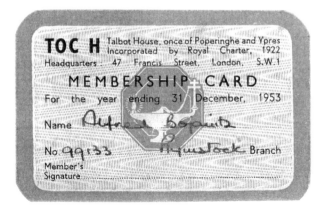

Left: TocH membership card illustrating the lighted lamp that kept people like Nellie aglow for good causes in their daily living. Of interest my father was 31 when he joined TocH in 1948.

My parents established and ran Wembury Youth Club. Some events are recorded in the souvenir programme of the opening of the Village Hall.

SOUVENIR PROGRAMME

Official Opening

of the New

WEMBURY
VILLAGE HALL

by

SIR HENRY STUDHOLME, Bt., c.v.o., M.P.

at **2.30** p.m.

Saturday, 28th July, 1956

PRICE - SIXPENCE

The old Village Hall, an ex-Army hut of 1914-18 vintage, was presented to the village in 1922 by the late Mr. Cory, of Langdon Court, who also provided the site.

This wooden building passed through various vicissitudes until in 1938 a start was made to raise funds for the building of a new Hall.

During the 1939-45 War large numbers of Service personnel were entertained in the Hall. Dances, cinema shows, concerts, etc., were held regularly—even during the progress of air raids.

Most of the building fund was obtained during the period of the war. The fund further increased by £300 from the money raised by the War Memorial Committee.

When in 1955 Government grants towards the cost of building village halls became available it was decided to proceed at once with the erection of the new Hall.

A Hall costing £4,200 was planned and an application for a grant of £1,400 was made to the Ministry of Education. Through the good offices of the then Mr. H. G. Studholme, M.P., Mr. A. H. Popham, National Council of Social Service, and the Devon Education Committee this grant was obtained.

Meanwhile, the invested capital, which is in Government Stock, has suffered serious depreciation, and at the date of opening there is a deficit of approximately £150 on the cost of the building.

Brief Description of the New Hall

Architect: Mr. W. ROSEVEARE, M. Inst. R.A.

Main Contractor: Messrs. W. COOPER & Son.

The building is a steel-framed structure of concrete block cavity walls on a solid brick and concrete base and is 65 feet long and 30 feet wide. The external walls are rendered in rough-cast down to floor level. The roof is of asbestos cement sheeting and fully ventilated. The main entrance leads to a vestibule with a kitchen on the left and ladies' and gentlemen's toilets on the right, while ahead lies the auditorium, having a permanent stage at the far end, with storage space below. The vestibule, kitchen, and toilets, which are fully equipped, have tiled floors and between the ceiling of this section and the roof is a storage space with access from the auditorium. The auditorium has a polished hardwood block floor and a suspended ceiling following the contour of the apex roof. On the left (facing the stage) is the emergency exit. The auditorium measures 38 feet by 30 feet and has a seating capacity of approximately 200. The stage is 13 feet deep and can be made the full width of the Hall by means of two moveable stair extensions. The proscenium opening is 8 feet high and 17 feet 6 inches wide. The end wall at the back of the stage has been left unfinished, as it is hoped to provide a billiard room extension behind the stage at some future date. The building is adequately provided with windows and there is electric lighting by globes suspended from the ceiling. The interior of the building and porches have been decorated in a variety of attractive and cheerful colours.

COMMITTEE OF THE WEMBURY VILLAGE HALL, 1956.

President and Chairman: Captain L. C. E. AYRE, C.B.E., R.N.

Vice-Chairman: Mr. W. E. BALL.

Hon. Secretary: Mr. L. ADAMS JONES, M.A.

Hon. Treasurer: Mr. J. H. WEBBER.

Mrs. BURROWES. Mr. BOJANITZ, Mrs. EVERITT, Rev. G. N. DAVIDSON, Mrs. JESSEP, Mr. J. EVERITT, Miss JONES, Mr. R. P. JESSEP, Mrs. ROWE, Mr. F. C. ROWLAND, Mrs. SPENCER. Mr. C. P. SOPPET, B.Sc.

Vice-Presidents: Mrs. AYRE, Mr. J. K. H. JOHNSON.

Caretaker: Mr. P. P. J. CRAGO, Church Road, Wembury

REGULAR VILLAGE HALL ACTIVITIES.

Youth Club.—Leaders: Mr. and Mrs. Bojanitz. Boys and girls under 16 years of age. Every Thursday.

Tennis Club.—Hon. Secretary: Mr. J. Everitt. Senior Section age 16 and over. Junior Section 14 and 15. Meetings throughout the summer at the hard court at Wembury House, which the Club is allowed to use by the kind permission of Sir Henry and Lady Studholme.

Whist Drives or Dances every Saturday night at 7.30. The Whist Drives held on the third Saturday of each month are organised by the Wembury Football Club.

News Letter.—The Wembury News Letter and Programme Parade was first issued in May, 1955, under the direction of the Village Hall Management Committee and edited by Mrs. Burrowes, of Wendy Cottage, Church Road, Wembury. The aim of this publication is to keep subscribers informed of details of all activities taking place in the Village. The subscription is 2s. 6d. per 12 monthly issues. If you are not already a subscriber, why not send 2s. 6d. to the Editor and have your name added to the mailing list?

Wembury now has a public building with which the residents should be well satisfied and which is suitable for functions of all kinds.

The Management Committee is commencing its work in these new premises handicapped by a debt of approximately £150. In order of priority the Committee aims to clear the debt as quickly as possible, cover working expenses and depreciation, and provide equipment in keeping with the new Hall. These objectives will be attained only if the Hall is used to capacity and if the residents give their full support. Please remember it is YOUR HALL. The Management Committee will organise functions, etc., for which a desire is expressed by residents and trusts that such functions will be well patronised.

The Hall is available for hire for much of each week at moderate charges and organisers of dances, whist drives, concerts, dramatic entertainments, whether in or out of Wembury, are invited to address enquiries to Mr. L. Adams Jones, Higher Howden, Beach View Crescent, Wembury, who will gladly give all information and help.

You may wish to have a children's party or a wedding reception—the new Village Hall is the ideal place. If you are the organiser of an outing from a place some distance away, why not consider a coach drive to Wembury, a bathe or ramble along the cliffs, and finish with tea and dance or whist drive in the Village Hall before returning home?

Outdoor Events
3.30-6.30 p.m.

Boys' and Girls' Races at 10-minute intervals. Entrance 1d. per race. Prizes. Organiser, Miss Maynard.

Skittles. Continuous. Prizes. Organiser, Mr. F. C. Rowland.

Putting. Continuous. Organiser, Mr. R. P. Jessep.

Lucky Dip. Continuous. Organiser, Mrs. Everitt. Everitt.

Treasure Hunt. Continuous. Prizes. Organiser, The Vicar.

Wheel. Continuous. Prizes. Organiser, Mr. A. Bojanitz.

Numerous Competitions.

3.30-3.40 p.m.—Comic Football Match. Organiser, Mr. Perrin.

4.0.-5.0 p.m.—Teas will be served by the Ladies' Committee. Choice of Snack Bar or Table Service. Ices and soft drinks.

Public address equipment kindly provided by Messrs. Moon and Sons (Pianos), Ltd.

BUSES.—The Western National Omnibus Co., Ltd., is providing augmented services between Plymouth and Wembury throughout the afternoon and evening and has arranged a special service for dance patrons, leaving Wembury for Plymouth at midnight. Normal fares.

The Management Committee wishes to thank all friends and supporters who have given prizes, refreshments, etc., or have helped in other ways.

CAR PARK.—A free Car Park is available adjacent to the Hall, but the Committee cannot accept any responsibility for any loss or damage arising from its use.

PROGRAMME OF EVENTS

2.15 p.m.—All present to assemble outside the Hall clear of the entrance. Fancy Dress Competitors line access to the entrance. Seats will be provided for older people.

2.30 p.m.—Sir Henry Studholme hands the key to the child who will unlock the door. The Chairman and Sir Henry, followed by the Committee, enter the Hall and take up position on the stage and the spectators gather in the auditorium. The Chairman introduces Sir Henry, whose reply will be followed by a vote of thanks. Blessing of the Hall by the Rev. G. N. Davidson, Vicar of Wembury. The child who unlocked the door receives a miniature of the key used. Miss Susan Johnson, on behalf of Mr. J. K. H. Johnson, is presented with the silver key used at the unlocking of the door. Judging of the Fancy Dress Competitors of school age. Sir Henry Studholme unveils the Coronation Seat, which has been provided by the Coronation Committee from surplus funds and presented by them to the residents of Wembury.

3.30 to 6.30.—Programme of outdoor events, details of which are given on the opposite page.

8.0 to 11.45.—Grand Dance to music provided by A. Holloway's Rhythm Band. Spot waltz. Admission 3/- (lower age limit 16 years). Running Buffet. Competition. Bus Service see opposite page.

BRICKS.—Have you bought a Book of Bricks? If not get in touch with the Vice-Chairman, Mr. W. E. Ball.

WEMBURY VILLAGE HALL YOUTH CLUB.

Balance Sheet for Year Ending 31.12.56

Expenditure	£	s	d
To Village Hall Subscriptions / Hire of Hall	13	15	3
" Electricity	2	12	6
" Refreshments		10	.
" Equipment	15	8	11
" Travelling, coach & part of training week-end	7	10	6
" Prizes and Gifts	31	10	4½
" Postage	6	17	1½
" Stationery		4	3
" Annual Subs. D.Y.C		19	2
" Insurance		5	.
" Caretaker (Mrs. Goldstone)	9	9	9
" Piano Removal	5	.	.
	2	5	.
	72	12	9½
Balance in hand		18	2
" at the Bank	10	.	.
£	93	10	11½

Income	£	s	d
Balance at 31.12.55			
Cash	8	16	9
Bank	3	10	2
By Taking Entrance, Coach trip and Refreshments	70	14	0
" Sale of Rackets		10	0
£	93	10	11

I have examined these accounts in accordance with the books and vouchers submitted and find them to be correct.

E.G. Purdy
Auditor

Madge Rundle, Winnie Symons.

10. Songs of the Moment

Entire Group and Audience

God Save The Queen

Photograph of the event .....

Everyone is ready to go in for the official opening. Sir Henry Studholme (left of the doorway) is about to enter the hall. The lady to the left of the officiants is Mrs. Lorum. Jennifer Everitt as 'Littler Bo Peep' peeps around Sir Henry Studholme. Reverend Davidson, well liked by the children of the parish, is easily identified by his 'dog collar'. Mr. Webber, who previously issued the pedal cycle certificate at

Above:
Children's Fancy Dress Parade.

Left: Six year olds Christine O'Connor
and Maria Bojanitz await the name of
the lucky winner.

Wembury Football Club in the 1950's

Back row: Jack Webber, ?, Mr. GIlbert, Mr. Beer, Joyce and Roy Burgess, footballers Brian Perring and Alec Eaton, Ernie Jewell, footballer Brian Sugden, Jack Everitt, footballers Ted O'Neil and Gordon Nicholls, Bert Wood, Herbert Spencer (in the striped jersey), footballer Mr. Vivien (?), Tim Craig, Mrs. Eaton and daughter, Pierre Louis.

Four ladies on the left of the photo: Beat Spencer, Mrs. Joyce Mugeridge, Mrs. Everitt, Alice Spencer.

Front row, left to right: Alfred Bojanitz (club secretary), Jimmy Everitt (child), Alf Perring, Frank (?), footballers Freddie Hopkins, Jack Laity, John Mugeridge, Mr. Hudson, John Chow. In the suits and ties: Denis Horwell (of the Jubilee Inn), Bob Adams.

A boy, Miss. Elizabeth Drake, Mrs. Eva Snell and Miss Howell (organist) present Christmas gifts for refugees to Reverend Davidson.

Cycling Proficiency test at Wembury Primary School, Ford Road.

The children are Roger Smith, David Jones, Paul Hocking, Paul Adams, Barry Greep, Robin Brown, Maria Bojanitz, the Headmaster and local Policeman. All the children passed their test to receive a certificate.

Photograph: Courtesy of the Evening Herald.

Left: Cub and Guide... Michael and Maria Bojanitz, 1961

Below: Edna's snapshot of Barry Stephens at the wheel of his Grandfather's tractor with Michael Bojanitz alongside.

In the Autumn of 2000 Barry told me the tale his grandfather Bob Philips often had told of the daring escape he and his brother Charlie had made from Guernsey where they had a farm. At night they stole a German motor boat and crossed the Channel to England. After the war Charlie returned to Guernsey whilst Bob and his sister Gilda remained in England. It would seem Gilda's status as an evacuee had rather unusual origins.

Wembury School pupils study the shore 1961

The children: Back row right to left ..... Gareth Jones, Roger Smith, Andrew Riddle, Barry Greep, ?, Paul Adams, Nichola Lugar, Paula Grieg, Robin Brown, Philip Brown, Maria Bojanitz, David Jones, Linda Louis, ?, Christine O'Connor, Alan Sperring, Geraldine Peel, Michael Bojanitz, John Grieg, and standing next to the Headmaster is Andrew Carn.

Photograph: courtesy of the Evening Herald.

Confirmation Candidates at St. Werburgh's Wembury
24th February,1965.

Photograph courtesy of The Evening Herald

Back row, left to right: Maria Bojanitz, Mary Everett, Nicholas Giles,Felicity Pursley, Dale Clifford, Fiona Norris, John Tomlinson, Yvonne Pursley.

Centre row: Left to right: David Fisher, Gareth Jones, Fiona Norris, Alan Taylor.

Front row, left to right: Mrs.Gwenda O'Connor, Mrs. Susan Wright of Down Thomas Post Office, Jennifer Giles, Susan Wright, Bishop of Exeter The Right Reverend Robert Mortimer, Mrs. Georgina Taylor, Mrs. Kathleen Andrews, Alan Taylor, ?

Perhaps someone can identify the unnamed young lady? Her name has been omitted on the church register of that time.

Mrs. Alice Mary Badcock seated at the organ at St. Werburgh's in 1965.

About the organists: Mrs. Badcock was organist at St. Werburgh's in the 1960's as was Mr. Dennis Baskerville (who ran the Wembury post office and then the Mill Cafe for a time). The current organ in the main body of the church replaced the organ that had been situated in the vestry. Before that time a harmonium was used. Later the harmonium was transported to the parish room where it remained for many years. Reginald Salmon who had been assistant organist at Bath Abbey succeeded Mrs Badcock. Miss Eileen Drake was a long serving choir member of some sixty five years or more. She was also a relief organist and organist at H.M.S Cambridge. She was a supply teacher at Wembury School and Sparkwell School for many years. Mrs. Badcock was a piano teacher and taught Maria and Michael and other children in the community.

Above: The wedding day of Janice Miller (Mrs. Badcock's daughter) to David Spiller 1965. Choir members are:

Back row: Left to right: Edna and Maria Bojanitz, Connie Atkins, Reverend Arthur Bromham, Michael Bojanitz (holding the crucifix), Eileen Drake, Michael Boyce, Hugh Jones. Front row: ? Cheetham (one of identical twins), Susan Boyce, Jane Richardson, Denise Little, Ann Smith, Hywell Jones (dark hair), Nicholas Cheetham (fair hair).

Below: The wedding day of Jacqui Rowland to Ian Gray 1967. Miss Maynard is to the left of Reverend Arthur Bromham.

Photograph courtesy of The Evening Herald

Pamela Soppet and Maria Bojanitz receiving their Queen's Guide award in 1965. Left to right: Sally Smallridge, Jill Butchers, Pamela Soppet, Mrs. Round (district commissioner), Maria Bojanitz, Ann Smith, Elaine Smith(not related), Fiona Norris.

Alfred's retirement photograph

(Evening Herald, 2nd September 1982).

In the news article my father (who had worked as a Betterwear salesman) is quoted as saying .... "I was in Russia on the German front as a runner for the German army. Later I was sent to fight Tito, and became an interpreter.

When the Americans arrived I was chucked into an aeroplane and eventually arrived at Kitley and came to Brixton where I met Edna who is now a car park attendant in Wembury".

During a Westward T.V street interview a few years before my father retired he was asked "Should Charles Church remain as a war memorial?" His spontaneous answer was "No, churches are for prayer and worship. English and German people should pray for each other". When Lily Steer married George Henry Sly in that same church in 1903 they could not have envisaged a future son in law, who had started out as a novice monk in Jugoslavia, upholding his conviction in some future time concerning their place of worship.

Edna and Alfred

A happy snap shot at Dartington, taken by Maria a week before Alfred's death in May 1991 ..... "My parents believed in a wonderful future beyond death. God bless them both and all who have contributed to this book. Perhaps this part of the collective human story serves as a window to a very special and traumatic period of history."